*Heal* America,
Heal Yourself
by Correcting
Your Habits

# *Heal* America, Heal Yourself by Correcting Your Habits

## Guidance for Preventing and Reversing Various Kinds of Diseases

By

Michelle Moore

Strategic Book Publishing and Rights Co.

Strategic Book Publishing and Rights Co.
12620 FM 1960, Suite A4-507
Houston, TX 77065
www.sbpra.com

For information about special discounts for bulk purchases, please conttact  Strategic Book Publishing and Rights Co. Special Sales, at bookorder@sbpra.net

ISBN: 978-1-62516-941-9

Book Design by Julius Kiskis

21 22 20 19 18 17 16 15 14    1 2 3 4 5

# Contents

# Acknowledgments

I would like to dedicate this book to those who have lost their lives as a result of medical malpractice. I also dedicate this book to those who have lost their lives due to rejection of appropriate care by insurance companies, and for those who have lost their lives just because they could not afford the medical care. Former President Clinton was shocked by the death rate from medical malpractice.

I also dedicate my book to my parents who supported my decision to study chiropractic medicine in this country. Both of them were my first patients and I could not help them so much when they were dying as I was far away from them. My father died from cancer and stayed in hospital care at his terminal stage. I adjusted him during my final visit. He acknowledged that I could eliminate his pain that the hospital doctors could not help at that time. I am also grateful for my friends, some of my patients, and my colleagues who encouraged and supported me to write this book. Most importantly, I am very thankful to my husband for his patience and support during this passageway.

**My intention in writing this book is to help you to minimize uncomfortable conditions and prevent early death from fatal conditions. I also hope you can save lots of medical expenses throughout your lifetime.**

**I have listed the title of movies you may want to watch and the titles of books you may want to read as references. I also listed some of the websites you may want to check out.**

# Introduction

He who has health has Hope, and he who has Hope has Everything . . . Arabic proverb

Health is the foundation for life; yet, we may experience dis-ease that is not pleasant at that time. Whatever the condition you may experience, it is not always negative if you can learn from the experience and withdraw positive conclusions such as compassion for others.

I came to this country to study chiropractic medicine from one of the Asian countries so that I could still maintain some Asian philosophy, religion, and belief systems from my background. I had a health hardship in my twenties that I overcame through chiropractic care, so I decided to become a chiropractor.

I had a blind trust in Western medicine. I thought a doctor could cure any health problem. I just needed to see a doctor whenever I had a health problem. I was very wrong. That was a big lesson for me. I realized that doctors diagnose and assist a patient to function in their daily activities. I also realized the only person who can cure the problem is the patient him/herself after traveling to so many specialists in my home country.

I experienced a tingling sensation below on my left chest while I was downhill skiing and noticed a problem in balance a little bit at that time. Within two weeks, the tingling sensation had become stronger and spread down to my left thigh. Within four weeks, the tingling sensation had become numbness and I experienced spastic paralysis in my entire left lower body, and it was spreading to my right lower leg. *I need to see a doctor . . .* I thought. Going to see a doctor induced a sense of fear, anxiety, nervousness, depression, some regret, and guilt for not taking better care of myself. I was aware of the complexity of those feelings; however, it was bad timing because it was the New Year holidays so that most places were closed to celebrate New Year's Day. My mother packed up my pajamas and underwear in a bag, as she expected the hospitalization to last for a while. We rushed into the major hospital right after New Year's Day, and I was referred to a neurosurgeon at the hospital and hospitalized immediately. The doctor told me that he would check from the top of my head to my toes. The team of neurosurgeons performed all kinds of exams on me as they tried to find out the cause. They spent three weeks completing the exams. Some of the examinations were very traumatic, such as a CT-scan, spinal taps, and so on. My father needed to authorize and to sign the forms at some of the examinations because they might have caused permanent damage to my nervous system or they had high risks of blah, blah, blah . . . I was scared and nervous. The X-ray technicians said, "Leave the room after you position the patient because it is dangerous!" I was left alone on the cold X-ray table in a gown, thinking, *Why do they leave a patient in a dangerous place? Well . . . I need the dangerous exams at this time.* After completing all the exams, they could not find anything wrong, so I was prescribed high dosages of steroid medications. The doctor told me, "This is the magic pill to cure your problem, shh." I observed the changes in my appearance as well as the side effects all over my body after a while. I also got acne all over my face by the time I could get out of the hospital.

During my hospitalization, I made some friends with fellow patients. The middle-aged man who had a similar condition as mine told me that he saw the orthopedic surgeon before I was hospitalized and he was in a wheelchair after the surgery. He could not leave the hospital when I could, even though my face was still full of acne. The neurology department was next to the oncology department at the hospital so that I talked with some people with cancer. We patients had meals in a big dining room together and I observed many of the patients had habitual patterns to eat meals. After I could get out the hospital, I consulted a dermatologist for my skin problem and he told me that acne that was a side effect of the medication; but, the dermatologist could not give me any more steroids. I was told to take vitamin C for my skin problem. I tried high dosages of vitamin C that did not help so much and I experienced fatigue. One of my sister's friends saw my face and referred me to a practitioner of Oriental medicine. He touched my back and applied multiple patches. He told me, "Your body is so toxic because of the medication you took, you must feel tired very easily," before I said anything about fatigue. He said the patches would create blisters overnight and he would break the blisters to take out the toxins from my system. It hurt a little bit when he punctured the blisters and when I took a shower afterward. I observed pus coming from the blisters. The acne over my face diminished and I was feeling better and better every day and he discharged me after ten days. The doctor told me, "This is what you need at this time although that is not for everything."

A couple years later, the side effects of the prescription resulted in more serious problems in my case. I was really upset with the neurosurgeon who gave me the medication and to myself because I lacked knowledge of medicine. I went back to see the neurosurgeon again and was told my condition was induced by the medication so they could not do anything. I was referred to another specialist, the orthopedic surgeon for that condition of bone destruction called avascular necrosis. I was told my condition was 99.9 percent incurable. The only solution was surgery to replace my hip joint; but, they could not guarantee my regular daily activities as I was still so young and active. I thought about a lawsuit against the doctor who gave me the medication, but found there was no chance of winning because it was the standard and appropriate procedure in Western medicine. I was so depressed and desperate and cried every day. My thoughts raced, *Do I need to give up my favorite downhill skiing? Do I need to quit my job because I need to walk and take packed trains to commute? Do I end up in a wheelchair for the rest of my life?* I felt I would need multiple bodies if I stayed under Western medicine because they had divided up my body parts. I didn't want to chop up my body for repair unless it was absolutely necessary. These questions came up one after another in my mind. The last question I came up with was, *Isn't there any doctor who can fix my problem?* I wanted to go back to the doctor in Oriental medicine and found he had passed away. I listed all sorts of alternative medicines and started looking for a doctor and expected to try one after another, whatever it took, however much it cost. Around that time, one of my co-workers told me that she saw a chiropractor. I had heard about chiropractic medicine and had the impression all they did was pop and crack backs and necks. I was afraid of it and asked her what he did.

She told me he did not pop or crack. "It's so gentle, but hard to describe . . . "

I wanted to check it out and try his chiropractic procedure. He gently touched my back and checked out my spine. I was amazed what he did on my body after the first adjustment. I felt much better and told him how I felt during his adjustment. He smiled at me and I felt a sense of hope and this made me smile. I saw him once a week for one year and I developed enough confidence to get back on my skies and I tried downhill skiing. I could do it even though I had some residual pain in my hip joint. The name of his office was "Eureka."

Life is a duality. There are always both positive and negative aspects. A fact itself has no meaning; it is neutral. We are the one to give meaning to a fact. We can withdraw a positive result from a negative incident. It all depends on how we view the facts, what we learn from the lessons, and how we interpret the incidents. Sometimes, we make mistakes and fall down, but oftentimes, we pick up ourselves as if nothing happened. Life is full of lessons to be learned to correct our lifestyle, our habits, and our viewpoints for our mental health that affects our physical health. We complete a growing phase at twenty-five years of age and we start the deteriorating phase after that age. As we age, we tend to develop physical problems as a result of the aging process in general. Yet, aging processes differ by each individual who has good habits and how a person takes care of his/her body. I learned that lesson so I changed my diet, do exercise, and quit some of my bad habits such as crossing my legs while seated and so forth, but I am not well-disciplined like a hyperactive kid. My mother nicknamed me "cockroach" when I was a teenager because I was active in the kitchen in the middle of the night. She later nicknamed me "bomb" because I was adventurous and sometimes shocked her.

I am so sorry, Mom; I caused your high blood pressure . . .

# Statistics

There are so many types of readings based on statistics such as numerology that has nine year cycles, the Chinese zodiac that has a twelve-year cycle, some say seven-year cycles, and so on. It seems that we have a certain cycle like a biorhythm. Nature has four seasons. Our life can be like four seasons by dividing up each section into twenty-five years. From birth to twenty-five can be like the spring time or a growing phase, between twenty-five and fifty years can be like summer, between fifty and seventy-five can be like fall or a harvesting time and we will have winter representing strength after seventy-five years. The following numbers are interesting statistics based on the Chinese zodiac based on astronomical statistics.

Age: The Chinese zodiac tells that women will have a disastrous year at age thirty-two starting one year before and ending at one year later. Between thirty-one and thirty-three, a woman may experience a health problem, a financial crisis, job related problems such as lay off, loss of a beloved one, or family problems. It could be the turning point of hormonal balance. The same type of turning point for men is forty-one years old so that a man may experience crisis between forty and forty-two years old. Some say that working women may experience a disastrous year like men, between forty and forty-two years of age.

The other says that people may have a troublesome year at the age before the changing of a decade, such as thirty-nine, forty-nine, fifty-nine, or sixty-nine. Some say that when the same numbers are aligned such as fifty-five or sixty-six, that these are bad years and leap years multiples of twelve such as twenty-four, thirty-six, forty-eight, sixty, and seventy-two are also disastrous.

Chinese people say "Avoid starting new things such as starting a business, changing a job, or building a house during certain periods of time or the year. Some say spending money to buy a car or a house will minimize the disaster."

People may experience a sprain/strain type of minor injury during the growing phase, but some active kids may experience head trauma that may manifest as more serious problems later in their lives. Young adults in their twenties and thirties may experience stiff necks, shoulders, or lower backs that become pain later. When a person hits the forties, he or she may experience more diagnostic conditions, such as high blood pressure, diabetes, high cholesterol, herniated discs, and so forth and many of them start taking prescriptions. Some people may experience more serious conditions, such as cancer or fibromyalgia in their thirties and forties. Some may go through surgeries for such conditions as ovarian cysts, hysterectomies, gall bladder, and so forth.

The fifties are another major declining period and some may have more surgeries for items, such as polyps in the colon, bypass surgeries in heart vessels, and so on. When a person hit the sixties, some may experience fatal conditions, such as a heart attack or vascular problems. In our seventies, incidences of heart attack, stroke, and cancer increase and many people go through surgeries and hospitalizations. Some of them may develop dementia, Alzheimer's, Parkinson's disease, or other neurological conditions in general.

Forty percent of those people who go into a bankruptcy do so because of medical expenses in the United States. Oops! It's increased to 65 percent! The bad thing is this is not considered as bankruptcy.

Forty percent of gun owners kill themselves.

Forty percent of cancers are prevented by changing lifestyle and diet. (According to research in England, some say 45 percent of cancers are preventable.)

Forty percent of medical expenses in the United States are spent by obese people.

Forty percent of the wealth in this country is controlled by 1 percent of the people.

Forty percent of the population in the United States maintains a standard body weight; the rest of them, 60 percent, are overweight.

The average life span of NFL players is forty-nine.

The average life span of medical doctors is fifty-nine years.

The average life span of chiropractors is sixty-nine years.

The average life span of regular people is seventy-nine years.

The average American experiences automobile accidents eight times in their lifetime.

Average people may have incidences in which a person may die or be killed by a major accident or fatal condition six times in their life span.

# Happy Planet Index

The **Happy Planet Index (HPI)** is an index of human well-being and environmental impact that was introduced by the New Economics Foundation (NEF) in July 2006. People in Costa Rica are the happiest people on earth two years in a row. Vietnam and Colombia follow after that out of 151 countries. I suppose the new female president in Costa Rica is working hard on the changes on male dominancy to provide more job opportunities for women. There is a difference between a man and a woman in thinking and abilities. Recent science has started to reveal some differences in brain functions, for instance the Broca's area that is responsible for speech is slightly larger in the female brain than the male brain. Men talk about sports, finances, and health, more limited topics. Women talk about everything and are good listeners. Women go into more details. *Men Are from Mars, Women Are from Venus* is an interesting book about the differences between men and women. Mars also represents wars. The last twenty centuries are symbolized as the male era and we are facing the new female era. Some other countries already have female presidents or more females are involved in government in many countries. Those are also interesting changes in the world and I saw different characters in each country.

When I visited New Zealand, I saw their lifestyle is much slower because they have so much nature and live on agriculture with primarily sheep. The major cities are similar to one another, there are some differences in buildings and they are busy, packed, but there were not many in New Zealand. They grow only organic foods, maybe for the citizens and it may not be for export. My impression when I visited Japan was that it was very clean, but packed into a compact size, particularly in downtown Tokyo, and it was really busy. They still have smoking areas in the bars, restaurants, coffee shops, even in the trains. Hong Kong and Korea are similar in a way; I could hear the noise of gambling on the streets, smoking, drinking, walking around the street market in the middle of the night. The lifestyles vary depending on each country and city. When I visited the Netherlands, I could smell drugs on the street. People appeared to be very happy from smoking, drinking, and singing in the bars. I found that the government advertises the standard price for the drugs on TV. I know that the Netherlands is extremely open and I do not support the illegal drugs, but do support medical marijuana. I attended a seminar in Amsterdam and joined the canal cruise after the seminar. I found the majority of European doctors were smoking while the majority of American doctors did not smoke. Some people may need those illegal or legal drugs, but I am concerned about the health hazard, particularly for young kids as it creates more problems. Concerning domestic violence and abuse, those young kids may have reasons to mask their pain from reality. Watching their parents' fights could be very painful for kids. Divorce and the murder of wives in the United States seems to be quite high. People are under so much stress that this may reflect why kids and adults go into drugs. Maybe some individuals who are under so much stress may need marijuana to calm down. I hear some celebrities die from illegal drug usage. Whitney Huston, for example, died from illegal drugs in 2012. Even though celebrities can earn lots of money, they feel a lot of pressure to go in front of so many audiences, and they don't have much privacy from the media and in the public. I feel so sorry for them. If people want to use those drugs for a medical purpose, for leisure, or to mask their unbearable stress, it would be acceptable.

I know everyone has different sets of values, different personalities such as shyness, sensitivities, different perceptions, and so forth that may turn into habitual patterns for stress management. Those legal or illegal drug usages are closely related with emotional stress to mask the pain and to escape from reality.

## Work, Mahjong and Tea: Hong Kong's Secrets to Longevity

*Agence France-Presse*

09-17-12

Covered in smog and cramped apartment towers, Hong Kong is not usually associated with a healthy lifestyle. But new figures show that Hong Kongers are the longest-living people in the world.

Hong Kong men have held the title for more than a decade and recent data show women in the southern Chinese city overtaking their Japanese counterparts for the first time, according to the governments in Tokyo and Hong Kong.

Hong Kong women's life expectancy rose from an average 86 years in 2010 to 86.7 years in 2011, while Japanese women's longevity was hit by last year's earthquake and tsunami, falling to 85.9 years, census figures reveal.

So what is Hong Kong's secret to a long life?

Experts say there is no single elixir, but contributing factors include easy access to modern health care, keeping busy, traditional Cantonese cuisine, and even the centuries-old Chinese tile game of mahjong.

-- Rolling stones gather no moss -- "I love travelling, I

like to see new things, and I meet my friends for 'yum cha' every day," Mak Yin, an eighty-year-old grandmother of six says as she practices the slow-motion martial art of tai chi in a park on a Sunday morning.

"Yum cha" is the Cantonese term to describe the tradition of drinking tea with bite-sized delicacies known as dim sum. The tea is free and served non-stop, delivering a healthy dose of antioxidants with the meal.

"My friends are in their sixties -- they think I'm around their age, too, although I'm much older than them," Mak laughs.

Mak's favorite food is steamed vegetables, rice, and fruit. Cantonese food is famous for steamed fish and vegetables -- dishes that use little or none of the cooking oils blamed for heart disease, obesity, and high cholesterol.

But before Mak enjoys her afternoon tea, she joins a group of elderly people for her morning exercise of tai chi, an ancient Chinese practice said to have benefits including improving balance and boosting cardiovascular strength.

A study published in the New England Journal of Medicine in February found that tai chi reduces falls and "appears to reduce balance impairments" in people with mild-to-moderate Parkinson's disease.

Another factor behind Hong Kongers' longevity, experts say, is work. While others long for the day they can retire and kick up their heels, many people in Hong Kong work well into their seventies and even eighties.

Hong Kong does not have a statutory retirement age and it is common to see elderly people working in shops, markets, and restaurants alongside younger staff.

"Many old people in our city remain working, that contributes to better psychological and mental health," Hong

Kong Association of Gerontology President Edward Leung says.

"For older people, a lot of them are stressed because they have nothing to do and they develop 'emptiness syndrome.' This causes mental stress."

Fishmonger Lee Woo-Hing, sixty-seven, says he could not bear to sit at home and do nothing. His inspiration is local tycoon Li Ka-Shing, Asia's richest man, who still runs his vast business empire in his eighties.

"If Li Ka-Shing continues working at the age of eighty-four, why should I retire?" asks the father-of-four during a break from his fourteen-hour shift at a bustling market in central Hong Kong.

"If I just sit at home and stare at the walls, I'm worried that my brain will degenerate faster. I'm happy to chat with different people here in the market."

-- 'Mahjong delays dementia' -- Hong Kong's cramped living conditions are famously unhealthy, fuelling outbreaks of disease and viruses including bird flu and severe acute respiratory syndrome (SARS) that have killed dozens of people.

The city's reputation won it the dubious distinction of a starring role in director Steven Soderbergh's 2011 disaster thriller, Contagion, about a deadly virus that spreads from Hong Kong to the United States.

But in the day-to-day habits of ordinary people, experts say Hong Kong is a great place to grow old.

A popular local way of keeping busy and meeting friends is mahjong -- a mentally stimulating tile game that can help delay dementia, according to aging expert Alfred Chan, of Hong Kong's Lingnan University.

"It stimulates the parts that control memory and

cognitive abilities. It helps old people with their retention of memory," he says.

The complex rules and calculation of scores make mahjong, also known as the Chinese version of dominoes, mentally demanding. But the social aspects of the four-player game are just as important.

"In mahjong you need to play with three other people. It is a very good social activity, you have to interact with each other constantly," says Chan, who has studied the game's effects on the wellbeing of elderly people.

"It is also a self-fulfilling game because if you win -- whether you play with money or not -- it gives you a sense of empowerment."

Mahjong parlors are popular in Hong Kong, and mahjong tables are a must at Chinese wedding banquets.

"I'm in semi-retirement. I work in the morning and hang out with my friends by playing mahjong in the afternoon," says sixty-seven-year-old tailor Yeung Fook, on the sidelines of a game in his modest garment shop.

"I'm happier when I work. It's boring to just sit at home."

Articles featured in Life Extension Daily News are derived from a variety of news sources and are provided as a service by Life Extension. These articles, while of potential interest to readers of Life Extension Daily News, do not necessarily represent the opinions nor constitute the advice of Life Extension.

In one of the old *Superman* movies, heavy alcohol drinkers and smokers seem like a symbol of a loser in this country. I know those habits are health hazardous, but those individuals may have reasons to go into and stay in these habitual patterns. It seems very discriminative for those individuals and creates more obese people. I heard the inhibition of smoking affected so much business in bars and restaurants. Creating smokers' bars and restaurants could be better than creating discriminations and more obesity. Since we cannot eliminate stress in our daily life, it is all an individual's choice. As long as you can control, it is all acceptable. Control means that you know when to stop. It is acceptable to drink and smoke as long as you can manage. Of course, I mean public safety is the priority. If a person is drunk, ignores a red signal, and crashes into another car or house, that is not acceptable. Leave the car and stay over long enough to sober up or take a cab to go back home. Smoking in the designated area is okay. From time to time, we get a good day and a bad day. That's life . . . it's okay as long as you control and enjoy your life. Even though we do have regulations, illegal drug usage among teenagers and workers is common in the United States. I have heard from HR directors that screening tests show many illegal drug users. I have seen teenagers gathered behind buildings passing around drugs. Most likely they are aware they may go to jail and lose their jobs. I believe illegal and legal drug usage is related to a self-destructive emotional pattern to mask and/or escape from their reality. Even though the United States has developed advanced entertainment businesses including Disneyland, movies, and so on, and has images of a joyful country, it is in the past that we had the good old days. However, the majority of US citizens are not happy as it was ranked 150th out of 178 countries in 2006. The United States is also called Prozac country because so many people are on antidepressant pills and many doctors prescribe it so easily. Is it related to high expectations for happiness? Are people more money oriented to become rich? Money cannot buy happiness, love, or health. Many lottery winners experience more trouble than happy stories. Everyone needs some money to maintain and enjoy their lives. Do we need more than that? What we need is different from what we want. We need good food, not rich food. We need a place to live, not necessarily a mansion. We need clothes to maintain our body temperature, not necessarily expensive designer brands, air conditioners, and heating systems depending on the areas we live. Many of us are dependent on cars, not necessarily very expensive, imported cars.

As long as I traveled through some other countries in the world, I never saw so much extreme obesity among regular people as in this country, except for Sumo wrestlers in Japan. I find more obesity among young kids and teenagers these days. Excessive eating is related to stress or emotional issues oftentimes. Many American people gain fifty to sixty pounds by recession of smoking. Concerning the rate of medical expenses for obese people, I don't really know if quitting smoking is good or bad. Yes, life is a duality. It has both good aspects and bad aspects.

### 'Skinny' on Obesity

**Saturday, September 22, 2012.** It's no longer a revelation that many Americans are overweight. Surveys and studies constantly make that point, and the most recent one from the Trust for America's Health and the Robert Wood Johnson Foundation was no exception. It said that 68 percent of American adults are overweight and that things may very well get worse.

Some may find the drumbeat of warnings about obesity a little hard to take. However, as we have seen in other areas, repeating a message often pays off. Anti-smoking campaigns that began in the 1960s have reduced the number of American adults who regularly use tobacco from 42 percent in 1965 to less than 20 percent today, according to the Centers for Disease

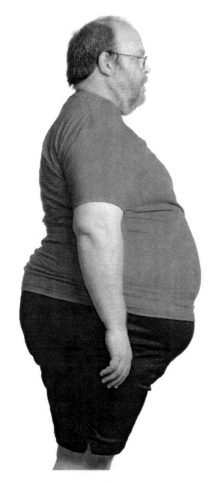

Control and Prevention.

Another remarkable thing in this country is so many lawsuits with many ridiculous ones such as the person burned by McDonald's coffee, which was settled with a small amount of money and medical expenses, but the law firm made a huge amount of money. The Lloyd's insurance company in England declined to cover insurance companies in the United States due to unbelievably ridiculous lawsuits in this country. There are so many unethical and greedy people who take advantage of the system. Are US citizens so desperate for money? Some of the regular people are desperate; many people cannot afford their own health insurance in the United States. Some may go into personal bankruptcy. Some of them lose their houses and jobs because of this outrageous medical and insurance system. Many small business owners and some companies have been modifying and cutting the budget for insurance. On the other hand, some of them take advantage of social security or welfare services.

I wonder if people in this country are more health oriented. Of course not, humans are all the same. We are all pleasure-seeking, fun-oriented, just different in appearance, in styles, and in thinking. Everyone is very unique genetically, biochemically, and in one's own experiences to develop one's own belief system. There is no replaceable value on each individual. You are very important to someone who loves you. Steve Jobs was diagnosed with pancreatic cancer at age forty-nine and passed away when he was fifty-six years old. He created multibillions and died at a young age. When we die, we separate from beloved ones and cannot take any money or a big house with us. Does it make your beloved one happier even though they receive lots of money? A mother of a young US soldier killed by the war may go into an alcoholic state to mask the pain. Is it blamable? Veterans suffer from nightmares for decades and may need marijuana. Is it acceptable? A single mother who may not be able to afford all her expenses may go into the prostitution business. Is it acceptable? Everyone has reasons for their choices to be happy, no matter if it is positive or negative. Do we have a higher expectancy to be happy? Do we need to buy a big house to be happy? Is it worth it to work like a work horse with so much financial pressure? Do we need to go on a luxurious vacation cruise every year? Of course not. If you can afford it, it is nice. Yet, the question is, are you controlling your money or is your money controlling you? Money is also very addictive. In many circumstances, I see that so many people are driven by money and all kinds of businesses became bad money games, which included some network businesses.

We all have different standards, sets of values, belief systems, lifestyles, and so on. Buddha stated that a life is tough and it is very true. What is happiness, then? We are all born to be happy. What makes us happy or unhappy? Is it similar to a glass with the water half-filled? It depends on how you view the glass, half-full or half-empty. Money can buy materials that may provide you temporary satisfaction to be happy. People keep on buying materials to get superficial happiness for a short period of time. Whatever the means you have for stress management, to minimize your frustrations, anger and irritations, people become obsessive so much so that they hurt themselves. Good examples are shopping to spend so much money and making their house cluttered, exercising to get a runner's high to raise endorphins and hurting themselves physically. People shift their addictions from one to another to release their emotional stress.

I would say, "Life is to enjoy!" One of my teachers gave me the book, *To Be Happy Is To Be Happy With.*" The author stated everyone is responsible for his/her own happiness and unhappiness. Pleasure would be doubled if you shared it with someone, sadness would be reduced if you shared with others. It is not easy to learn how to get along with another person to live with them. Marriage is tough; working with a nasty boss is tough. Everyone has family dynamics that are either functional or dysfunctional. Family dynamics are one of the toughest to deal with if it is dysfunctional. *Celestine Prophecy* is about emotional controlling patterns that we learn from our parents and describes about energy. Human relations are similar to a mirror image so that if someone is not nice to you, you may not be nice to that person. One of my favorite tales based on Buddhism is called, "Long Chopsticks in Heaven and Hell," which says that there is a huge dining table with a lot of good food on the top of the table in hell. Everyone at the table is given a pair of long chopsticks. People in hell pick up food and try to eat it by him/herself; however, the chopsticks are too long to feed themselves. So the people in hell struggle, hitting each other, and fighting all the time. They are starved and never happy. On the other hand, people in heaven have the complete same situation. They realized that they can pick up food, but they cannot feed themselves. Therefore, people in heaven feed each other and are happy all the time. Human relationships should be reciprocal. You can create a hell or heaven depending on how you act under the same situation. My husband's former boss is a multi-millionaire with a scar from trying to commit suicide, and he got divorced which resulted in the loss of a great deal of his money. One of my patients is wealthy, but she is isolated and lonely which resulted in major depression. I see many unhappy, rich people.

## ✻
# Electromagnetic Waves /
# Electromagnetic Fields

*Year 2001* and *Year 2011* are the classic movies about space travel. When the astronauts had trouble, the super computer named HAL (one letter in front of the letters that make up the name of the major computer company known as IBM) took control over the captain's own decision to save the crew. It is ironic because we are controlled by computers these days and we are in that period now. Super computers are created and compete by their speed and capacity. Watson, a super computer, has a feature to think and learn and is being utilized in the stock market and medical field. Seventy percent of the stock market is operated by computers that resulted in the "Flash Clash" that destroyed a company's stock price as it fell from $24.79 down to $0.01 in four seconds. The K computer, created by Fujitsu in Japan has a feature that calculates and selects the right protein binding factor medication for a particular individual in one day. This used to take months. Sequoia, in California, created by IBM has speed twice as fast as the K computer. So many things are automated and make our life easier and quicker, but sometimes it is a disaster. For instance, it has created different problems including crimes through the Internet, labor issues, and increased work load on individuals and so on. Silicon Valley in California imported people from China and India during the bubble economy so it is known that Silicon Valley is supported by the IC, or people from

India and China. IBM hires autistic people who can work sixteen hours straight without taking a break. It has the highest incidence of autistic kids in that area. They are creating humanoids, a 0, 1, 0, 1 Yes, No, Yes, No, so they work like a robot! An avatar can be on the corner. California has the highest incidence of autism, a 300 to 400 percent increasing rate, particularly in Silicon Valley. Why in California? I found out Arthur Clark, the author of *2001*, thought about the satellite positions, first. Three satellites to cover the whole earth for telecommunications, TV programs, weather satellites, and so on. He regretted that he did not apply for the patent on that idea. Possibly, the edge of this continent may get concentrated electromagnetic waves or radiation from the satellites. I don't know.

Human desires never end so that our culture has been developing well.

As I mentioned earlier, it works on both the positive and negative, so that while we have been advancing our culture, people are more dependent on electronic devices and we have lost our own ability. For example, we use calculators, or computer programs to calculate numbers when we punch in. It is quick and easy; however, many CPAs are losing their left brain function for calculation. We lose our own ability to memorize the name of the streets if we are dependent on GPS, phone numbers, and so on. The "use it or lose it" application is true for not only muscles, but also brain functions. In the last century, we developed so many new technologies, much more than the previous nineteen centuries. Particularly, the creation of electric and electronic equipment is very remarkable. However, there are various diseases, so called idiopathic diseases or syndromes, which we cannot find a cause to which have been increasing along with the electric and electronic device development.

Our brains are operated by an electric current that exchanges plus and minus ions to create synaptic voltage to connect neurons. Even though scientists cannot conclude cordless phones and cell phones directly affect our brain, it could result in brain tumors. We have a lot of neurons in our brain and we kill many neurons every day depending on how we use our brain and how we nourish and activate the brain. Our brain needs oxygenation, good nutrition, such as good sources of protein like fish, poultry, eggs, and some glucose. Our brain also requires activation to maintain its function. Many people can feel the electromagnetic waves (EMW) from the cell phones. Cordless phones used to use megabytes, but we use gigabytes these days, a one thousand times higher frequency than the megabyte that is the unit the majority of electronic devices use for its memory unit. When I attended a seminar, the instructor checked the EMW of cell phones so that many people gathered around the instructor and started calling numbers that emit EMW at a high level. I was in the middle of the group to be checked out my cell phone's EMW along with the electromagnetic absorber called Zeropa. Gee! I felt my brain move inside my skull and I could not stay in the room after that. As my brain was moved and cooked up, I felt my cranium was moved along with it so that I felt my face was like a Picasso art piece. I could not think clearly for a while and needed to have cranial work after that. It was a kind of rare situation because not so many people around us call up from their cell phones at the same time, but think about the usage of cell phones for a long period of time or frequent usage. Your brain reacts to the EMW, no matter if you are aware of it or not. I know I am very sensitive to many things so I need to check out if my perception is normal or abnormal sometimes. I looked around at the other people, and nobody reacted like me. Probably, I have an AB-normal brain. The other instructor stopped me and told me, "I am sensitive to EMW, too. You need to know how to protect yourself" and showed me a Q-wave pendant to wear. If you keep your cell phone(s) in the front pocket of your pants, this habit is very common among young boys/guys, sperm immobility may be induced, resulting in infertility.

Not only cell phones or cordless phones have electromagnetic waves; we are exposed to EMW emitted through computer screens and TV screens that we sit in front of for hours or all day long. Flight attendants and women who sit in front of computers all day long have higher incidences of infertility or miscarriage. Hair dryers, microwaves, electric cars, including hybrid cars, ceiling lights, and Smart meters for electricity and all sorts of electronic devices emit EMW.

Recommendation:

- Minimize the usage of cell /cordless phones and use a device or earphone to absorb or transfer the EMW or earphone. This way would save your phone bills as well.
- When you use a microwave, stay away from it, at least ten feet, while it is operating.
- Minimize use of microwaves as much as possible. Free radicals can be created by microwave cooked foods.
- For computer or TV screens, use an EMW absorber or another kind of device.
- Do not keep your cell phones in the front pocket of your pants.
- Minimize use of cell phones while you are driving, even if it is hands-free.

When I call a phone number, I get an automated announcement to select the service; I have to wait so long to get my job done oftentimes. Where is the service representative? What kind of service is it? Sometimes, service representatives are in another country. Even though they speak English, it is hard to understand strong accents. That automated system cut so much employment and they are still developing more technologies that would cut more employment. Some people say that 50 percent of white collar jobs may be cut in the near future. At certain points, many people think CPAs will not be necessary in the near future; yet, there are different kinds of problems that come with automated systems such as skimming, so that there are actually more demand on CPAs.

When I rushed into a bathroom at the airport, I placed a seat cover and the flash sensor reacted so that I grabbed the cover and sat. It reacted again while I was sitting there and splashed my butt twice! I laughed so hard in the bathroom by myself so it was very embarrassing to go out. I looked around if anyone was in the bathroom. Then, I put my hands under the faucet, water did not come out. I moved to the other sink and washed my hands. The paper dispenser's sensor did not respond and I waved many times, but it still did not respond and I ended up wiping my hands over my pants. I don't know how sensors will respond. Computers and new cell phone icons are convenient, but it sometimes gives me disaster and frustration to keep up with it and it costs so much money. I don't like the automated system in many ways. Oh, I am getting classic!

# THE CANCER RATE IS GETTING CLOSE TO 50 PERCENT

Some researchers predict that the cancer rate will increase up to 50 percent by the year 2020. It is approximately getting close to 40 percent or over these days. There are some areas or other countries that have already hit 50 percent. Although women worry about breast cancer and men worry about prostate cancer, the highest incidence of cancer is lung cancer even among non-smokers. Probably you have already noticed that more young people are diagnosed with cancer in their thirties and forties these days. Dietary factors are huge for these diseases, along with emotional and mental stress.

Some cancer patients with lung, skin or Hodgkin's (cancer of the lymph glands) could possibly reverse these conditions by having 4 table spoonfuls of pureed asparagus in the morning and again in the evening over a month period. Some of them were told by the doctor that their cancer was hopeless. You may need to adjust the dosage and duration up to one year or longer depending on the stages. Use cooked organic asparagus and put in blender to make puree. You can have it that way or dilute with cold or hot water and then drink it. For prevention, you can have 2 table spoonfuls of asparagus puree either that way or make a drink with water. Another possible way to prevent lung and prostate cancer is to eat more tomatoes. Greece is ranked as one of the top three in the world for the number of smokers; but, has a low incidence of lung cancer possibly due to its heavy consumption of tomatoes. Another possible way to prevent cancer is to have three raw almonds every day according to Edger Casey.

Because of the development of modern technologies, our life is speeding up and is more stressful than ever. The economic depression worldwide also increases the additional stress and work load on each individual. Moderate amounts of stress can have positive effects to increase workability, achievement, and management. Oftentimes, stress is created by ourselves by means of our own viewpoints, set of values, time management, and so forth. There are numerous books about good habits you may want to read. Our bodies react to various types of stress no matter if we are aware of it or not. These stresses are not only emotional and mental, but also chemical, thermal, EMW, micro-organisms such as bacteria, air pressure changes, altitude, and so on. Emotional and mental stresses are the major ones to control as well as our behaviors leading to habits. How we manage our stress may become our lifestyles: exercise programs, watching TV or movies, cleaning house, eating favorite foods, drinking/ smoking, gambling, shopping, and so forth. Chemical stress that involves what you eat and drink, what you use for skin care or make-up, direct contact with household cleaners, soaps, sun tan or sunscreen lotions, even taking a shower, swimming in a pool, or soaking in a Jacuzzi tub that contains huge amounts of chlorine that is carcinogenic, meaning cancer-inducing. Thermal stress as temperature change is also another stress to the body because human bodies are regulated to maintain a constant body temperature. Physical stress includes gravitational stress and postural stress, your own body weight, particularly to weight-bearing joints: ankles, knees, and hip joints because these joints support your entire body weight when standing and walking. The song, "the foot bone connects to a shin bone, the shin bone connects to a knee bone . . . " is very true. The other important weight-bearing joints are called the SI (sacroiliac) joints that are located on both sides of the body and connect the sacrum, which is located in the center of your buttock area, to the pelvic bones by ligaments. The entire spine sits on top of the sacral bone. The name of the bone, sacrum, is derived from the word, sacred. It is very sacred because that is the location of the autonomic nervous system that consists of both sympathetic and parasympathetic nervous systems. The sympathetic nervous system is also known as the fight or flight nervous system. It is activated by various stressors that control heart rate, capillary constrictions, sweat gland activations, muscle constriction, and so on. When you are under stress, such as being really mad or extremely frightened, your heart rate increases, you feel cold or even have a trembling type of reaction, which are good examples of this nervous system. The other nervous system is called the parasympathetic nervous system that works when you are relaxed and digesting your foods so that it makes you sleepy after you eat or relax. Eating, drinking, and smoking activates this nervous system and it works together along with the sympathetic nervous system. Smoking cigars or cigarettes gives a sensation of relaxation in spite of the excitation effects of nicotine that is due to activation of this nervous system and neurotransmitters called dopamine inside the brain that give you the sensation of relaxation and pleasure. Our brain receives signals from this autonomic nervous system through the spinal column constantly to maintain the balance and to regulate those functions. The brain and spinal cord are called the central nervous system. It is the main nervous system to control our body and life. The nerves branching off from the spinal cord to the arms, legs, and organs are called the peripheral nervous system. Let me explain how our bodies work together briefly. I believe the digestive system controls the chemical balance mainly on top of direct skin contact materials. Starting from the mouth, in a strict sense, visuals and smells activate the digestive system to secrete saliva. Food is chewed to break it down into small pieces. Do you chew food well? Do you chew on one side? Gobbling foods and chewing on one side are habits that contribute a tremendous effect on the digestive system and TMJ (jaw joints) that may affect other body parts. Then, the food goes down to the stomach and mixes up with the stomach juice that is called hydrochloric acid, to break down and liquefy foods. As we age, secretion of hydrochloric acid reduces so that we cannot eat our favorite foods as much as we used to eat at a young age or our food orientation may change by aging. The gall bladder secretes bile to break down fatty foods and the pancreas secretes digestive enzymes to break down foods, making insulin and glucagon to control our blood sugar levels. Then the food goes down to the small intestines and they absorb all sorts of nutrients that are carried all over the body through the bloodstream. Then, those foods go into the colon that absorbs water and excretes the unnecessary materials as feces. Those absorbed nutrients go into various chemical reactions carried into various body parts through the blood. This is a basic physiology of the digestive system. The central nervous system, digestive system, immune system, and endocrine system work together like four-wheel drive cars because of the chemical reactions in the gut. The majority of neurotransmitters produced stay in the gut and play a major roll for the nervous system. The enzymes inside the gut regulate the immune system and fatty materials are broken down to form hormones. Therefore, the gut is considered the second brain. One of my friends went on a no-fat diet to lose weight and ended up with major depression because it is all connected. Our body needs all kinds of nutrients. The highest death rate in the United States is still from heart attacks because we still eat very fatty foods, a steak and potato diet, a very typical American diet on top of fast foods; the average American eats nineteen pounds of French fries per year. However, the cancer death rate may exceed the heart attack death rate soon.

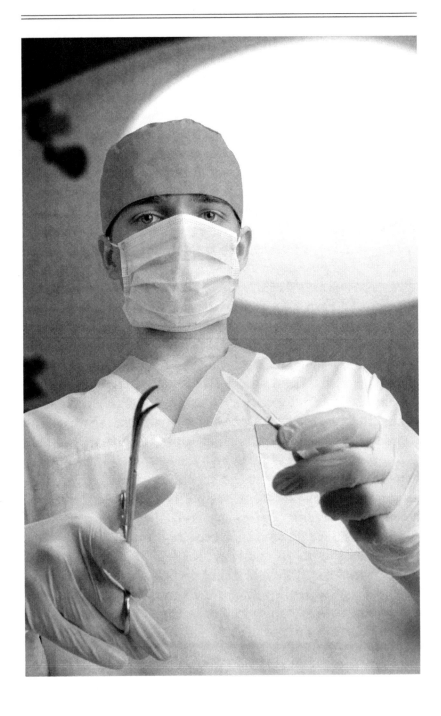

Hitting Cancer from All Sides

*PRNewswire*
    08-20-12
    SANTA ROSA, Calif., Aug. 20, 2012 /PRNewswire/ -- Cancer may be the Harry Houdini of diseases--it often finds devious ways to escape treatment. Because cancer disables our cellular quality control mechanisms, rampant mutations that cause tumor cells to grow uncontrollably can also generate resistance to anticancer drugs. Even if 99 percent of the tumor is destroyed, that 1 percent can come roaring back. How do we knock out that 1 percent? By attacking the cancer from multiple angles, using multiple treatments and strategies.

    "We need to outsmart the cancer before it outsmarts us. To do this, we have to find ways to attack cancer from many angles, so it doesn't have the opportunity to develop protective mutations," says integrative medicine pioneer, Isaac Eliaz, M.D.

    Recent research has demonstrated a variety of multipronged approaches to defeat cancer resistance. One study found that a sophisticated botanical formula restricts the aggression of metastatic breast cancer. The in vivo study, conducted by researchers at Indiana University and published in Oncology Reports, showed that a combination of medicinal mushrooms, botanical extracts, the flavonoid quercetin, and 3, 3'-Diindolylmethane (DIM) slowed highly aggressive triple negative breast cancer.

    The formula significantly decreased tumor growth and breast-to-lung metastasis. The cancer metastasized to the lungs in only 20 percent of the treated group, compared to 70 percent of the untreated group. Also, in the treatment group that did metastasize, the number and size of the lesions was dramatically reduced. Significantly, these results were achieved with no toxic side-effects.

The formula's success against cancer may, in part, be due to the independent, anti-cancer properties of each ingredient working together to create a synergistic effect. On their own, medicinal mushrooms *Trametes versicolor, Ganoderma lucidum, Phellinus linteus* have been shown to reduce cancer growth and invasiveness. Extracts from the botanicals *Scutellaria barbata, Astragalus membranaceus* and *Curcuma longa* induce programmed cell death (apoptosis) and reduce cancer metastasis. *Quercetin* reduces cancer cell proliferation and helps suppress tumor growth. DIM, an active component of cruciferous vegetables, reduces cancer growth, migration, and invasiveness.

Another natural anti-cancer agent, modified citrus pectin (MCP), gives the botanical formula even more power against cancer. In a groundbreaking study published in the journal, Integrative Cancer Therapies, MCP, a type of citrus pectin modified for enhanced anti-cancer effects, significantly boosted the anti-cancer actions of the botanical breast formula. When co-administered together, MCP significantly increased the breast formula's anti-cancer action, further reducing metastasis in highly invasive breast cancer. In the study, low concentrations of the formula decreased cancer cell migration by 21 percent. However, when co-administered with MCP, researchers observed a 40 percent decrease.

Another synergistic study paired MCP with the chemotherapy drug Doxorubicin (Dox). Published in the journal, *Cell Biology International,* the study found that combining Dox with MCP increased the anti-cancer activity of both agents. This finding bodes well for many cancer patients, especially those too weak for normal chemotherapy regimens, as combination therapy may allow for lower doses of Dox with enhanced clinical impact and reduced toxicity.

"The common thread through all these studies is that anti-cancer regimens with multiple modes of action increase treatment effectiveness," says Dr. Eliaz. "We are learning that the combination of therapies can be greater than the sum of their parts and that dynamic botanical formulas with different targeted ingredients can improve cancer care and reduce side effects."

For more information on the specific breast health formula studied call (707) 583-8619, email info@betterhealthpublishing. com, or visit www.BreastHealthFormula.org.

Source: Jiang J, Thyagarajan-Sahu A, Loganathan J, Eliaz I, Terry C, Sandusky GE, Sliva D. Breast Defend prevents breast-to-lung cancer metastases in an orthotopic animal model of triple-negative human breast cancer. Oncol Rep. 2012 Jul 26. doi: 10.3892/or.2012.1936.

About Better Health Publishing:

Better Health Publishing (BHP) focuses on the publication of key works promoting health and wellness. BHP believes that education and accessible information are the core components of a healthy and sustainable society.

"This news release was issued on behalf of Newswise(TM). For more information, visit http://www.newswise.com."

Better Health Publishing
CONTACT: Media Questions/Interviews with Dr. Isaac Eliaz, +1-707-583-8619,info@betterhealthpublishing.com
Web site: http://www.BreastHealthFormula.org/ Copyright PRNewswire 2012

*Economics* **magazine in the August 2012 issue also talked about cancers; they found that we need to views cancer from a different angle to treat them effectively.**

## HABITS

There are so many different types of habits we do on a daily basis that may lead to a health problem later. Once you realize your habits, it is no longer a habit. It becomes your choice.

*Food Inc.* is a movie about how foods are prepared, grown, and produced. *Super Diet* is another interesting movie about a fast food diet and about how it affects our organs.

There are various diets to maintain health, to lose weight, to shape a body as well as mentality. What we eat determines these factors. There are the Atkins diet, the blood type diet, the vegetarian diet, the macrobiotic diet, and so on. The body type diet by Transformation Enzyme Co. is quite interesting. I took the seminar about the body type diet. They classified four body types. The typical men's bigger upper torso is associated with a high protein diet. They crave red meats to maintain big muscle mass so they tend to develop high cholesterol problems and tend to get colon cancer unless they eat many more vegetables. People whose lower bodies are bigger than their upper bodies love fatty foods so that they tend to develop hormonal problems and breast cancer because hormones are made of fat. People who have a big belly and porky buttocks love carbohydrates so that they tend to develop pancreatic problems including pancreatic cancer. People with young-looking faces, are short, with evenly distributed fat, love dairy products and tend to develop neurological disorders. Good examples are Michel J. Fox with Parkinson's and Tom Cruz with dyslexia. Dr. DicQie Fuller PhD, DSc, is a pioneer on enzyme therapy in this country. She herself suffered from cancer in her early lifetime and stayed in Western medicine and developed different cancers repeatedly so that she changed her diet to a vegetarian diet and studied digestive enzymes in Germany. She brought back the concept to the United States and created the enzyme company. I remember Miss Universe was working for the company to shape her body around that time. There is a joke, "I need to eat a thin person." Diet affects not only body types, but also our mentality. Japanese monks maintain a very mild vegetarian diet so that their mentality is very mellow. People who eat spicy foods oftentimes seem to be more aggressive. Food itself is a medicine to supply nutrients to our body like gas to run a car. The question is if the foods contain enough nutrients or not. The FDA does not regulate the label on how those foods are produced such as genetically manipulated products as corn, soybeans, canola oils, and so forth or whether hormones are injected. It is scary to not know how safe our foods are these days. We may not be eating safe, nutritious foods in comparison to the past. Some researchers reported that the amount of nutritional values in produce has declined about 50 percent in comparison to the values of the same produce fifty years ago. We have been destroying the soil by spraying pesticides and chemical fertilizers to grow faster and bigger and look better. As a result, we cannot supply enough nutrients from our foods any more.

Diet: Our bodies need a variety of nutrients such as carbohydrates, protein, fat, vitamins, and minerals.
Rule 1. Eat organic items as much as you can afford or go to farmer's markets.
Rule 2. Eat raw foods as much as you can because enzymes are killed by heat.
If you eat cooked foods, take digestive enzymes along with

your meal.

Rule 3. Avoid white food such as white bread, white rice, and white sugar.

Rule 4. Eat fiber-rich foods such as eggs, dairy, veggies, and fruits for breakfast.

Rule 5. Avoid processed and fast foods as much as you can.

Rule 6. Drink eight glasses of water a day or 1/2 fluid ounce for each pound of your body weight.

Rule 7. Avoid any artificial sugar, margarine, etc. The body does not like it.

Rule 8. Avoid charcoal on your BBQ or grilled foods as much as you can.

Think about the "French Paradox . . . " French people drink a lot of wine and eat a lot of butter. In spite of their high amount of fat consumption, their cholesterol is not a really big problem in general, but this is not always true. They also have different dietary habits as they eat a big lunch and a small dinner. Many people eat big dinners in the evening or at night that may cause less calorie consumption during sleep. A recent study about the high potency of antioxidants such as resveratrol made from grapes activates certain parts of DNA that are usually dormant. The activation of DNA rejuvenates the cells, leading to more energy. Either taking resveratrol or eating a low calorie diet activates the part of the DNA strand. Resveratrol is one of the high potent antioxidants that are supposed to fight cancer, diabetes, Alzheimer's and other conditions. Glutathione is a precursor of the antioxidant and has lots of potential to work on those conditions and thyroid conditions.

There are so many different eating and drinking habits; that's the way you love it.

For example, sprinkling salt is one of the habits I see a lot, even before tasting the food, indicating stomach problems, and this habit increases the risk for high blood pressure. Eating ketchup over salted French fries is also high salt consumption.

Dipping sushi into soy sauce as much as the rice will absorb until it falls apart is bad as soy sauce contains a lot of sodium as well.

Sometimes, butter or peanut butter is spread thick on bread that increases the risk of high cholesterol, a fatty liver, or gallstones.

Many packages of artificial sweeteners are used to drink coffee or tea that may lead to some cancers. I recommend Stevia as other kinds contain junk chemicals if you use a lot.

**Posture:** Crossing your legs, hunching over, slouching, weighing on one side, and your sleeping posture, especially if you sleep on your stomach so that your neck is turned to one side, can affect your body. If you cannot sleep on your back or on your side, there is a donut-shape pillow for those people.

If you tend to sleep on one side, your shoulder joints will be compressed, even though the side posture, such as the fetal position with both legs bent up and both knees bent eases your lower back pain. Those positions may be indicative of what your body is compensating for. "Who cares? I cannot sleep with a different position!" Yes, that's right. We, Asian people believe sleeping with the left side down means that you have pancreatic issues and sleeping with the right side down means stomach problems. Kids move around during sleep to relax the muscles that they used that day. One morning, I woke up and realized my body was ninety degrees rotated on the king-size bed so that I had kicked out my husband from the bed. Yes!

Your body knows what to do. Over a long period of time, for a long term, it will create structural imbalance. A person who shakes his/her leg while seated is enhancing the pumping mechanism to circulate CSF (cerebrospinal fluid) indicating sacrum fixation. Babies and toddlers suck nipples and thumbs, putting pressure to lift up the hard palate that releases the intracranial pressure. Your body knows what to do.

**Punctuality**: Time management is habitual. I have not been good at this since kindergarten.

Oftentimes, it creates mental stress for driving, missing flights, losing jobs, etc. and may cost you a lot of money for traffic tickets or even your life if you should get involved in a major accident. I drive my husband crazy when he gives me a ride because he needs to race to the airport to catch a flight. I never learn . . .

**Carrying personal items:** With a heavy purse or briefcase over a shoulder, we tend to carry those items over the same side of the shoulder. A backpack or briefcase with wheels is better to carry heavy stuff.

Men often carry their wallets in the back pocket of their pants. The wallet contains many cards would produce thickness that gives pressure to the buttock area, often over the SI joint. Sometimes, they may sit over the thick wallet that is similar to sitting on an uneven surface causing pelvic torsion. The incidence of lower back pain is higher in men and is not necessarily heavy labor induced. When you are driving and step on a gas or brake pedal, it may compress the SI joint on the side you keep the wallet.

Another problem is carrying a cell phone in the front pocket of the pants as I mentioned earlier. When the cell phone rings, it emits a lot of electromagnetic waves (EMW). The location of the cell phone is close to the testicle so that it may result in sperm immobility. You may want to use a clip-on device to wear on your belt or wear a fanny bag.

**Smoking, drinking alcoholic beverages and drugs**: Those habits are related to emotional suppression. Even the majority of people know that these habits are health hazardous habits, but people still continue those habits.

Drinking as long as you are under control is acceptable. Being under control means drinking a glass of wine or beer. Drink lots of water or wait after drinking and there will be no stumbling, no fighting, no crying, no crashing, no throwing up and you'll be able to drive. The United States has a history of prohibition of alcohol. People had fights, created illegal alcohol breweries and sales; the Kennedy family created their wealth by that. Prohibition of those drugs may result in violence, crimes, and so on. Drinking masks the pain, so some people use alcohol as a painkiller for both physical and mental pain. Sometimes, grief may induce alcoholics. Heavy drinking on a regular basis may end up with liver problems and death. Drinking is linked with DNA in the brain so that some people cannot drink any alcohol. Maybe those people missing DNA are unlucky to enjoy life. Native American Indians have high incidence of alcoholic problems; a mother of a young American soldier who was killed by a war may turn to alcoholic. I don't blame them. Those are very hard habits to break due to emotional issue involvement. There is a Japanese proverb, drinking sake (Japanese rice wine) three ounces a day is a medicine for longevity. Japan is famous for longevity and its healthy diet, except for its high salt content soy sauce. If you drink regularly, I recommend you take a day off to give your liver a break and take vitamin B complex to break down the alcohol. Although I do not encourage you to smoke or drink, if you drink or smoke on the regular basis, my recommendation is to detoxify your system with a potato patch or other products to detoxify your system. Not only smokers or drinkers, the majority of us are so acidic and toxic. The following detoxification is very simple, safe, and inexpensive. I will list other detoxification programs later.

DETOX your system:
Potato Patch
*1 Taro potato, dark brown fuzzy potato, about the size of a fig

--- peel and grate (you can chop it up and use a food processor to make like a mashed potato. If you cannot find a taro potato, you can substitute a regular white potato. If you use the white potato, about the size of 4 inches long, you need to adjust the amount of ginger root, three-four times the size of your thumb).

*Ginger root (one joint size of your thumb, about a half of your thumb if you use one taro potato) grated (not necessarily peeled).

*Flour 1 tablespoon

1. Mix all ingredients well and make a paste.
2. Fold a paper towel in half and put the paste over the half of the paper towel.
3. Fold the paper towel so that the potato paste is covered like a sandwich.
4. Apply the potato patch over your liver and kidneys.
5. Put additional folded paper towels over the potato patch.
6. Cover up with a towel to wrap around the bottom of your rib cage and tie with a belt or a string.
7. Keep the patch on overnight and sleep with it.

***** The liver is a big organ. So, put the potato patch, about the size of your hand, let's say five to six inches from side to side, three to four inches high in an oval shape, on the liver. The liver is located at the bottom of your rib cage on the RIGHT side at the FRONT.

***** The kidneys are located at the bottom of your rib cage on both sides about one inch away from your spine on your BACK. So, make the paste about the size of your palm, let's say three inches side to side, four inches high, in an oval shape. Put one oval shape paste on the half of the paper towel and put another one about three to four inches apart that covers your spine.

***** Make the potato paste with three to four taro potatoes or more, three to four times that of ginger root and flour with the same ratio at one time so that it will supply you for four to five days. Keep it refrigerated.

Cautions: If you know that you have sensitive skin, you may have allergic reactions to the potato or adhesive tapes. I highly recommend trying this method with a small portion over the inner part of your thigh or forearm to test it. If you get an allergic reaction such as skin irritation or skin rash, please stop and consult with a dermatologist if it persists. Switch to the different detox methods or programs. I recommend not using adhesive tapes. If you love fast foods, you may want to add paper towels or towels not to stain your sheets.

**For hyperthyroid patients including Grave's disease:** You want to apply to cover up your spleen in addition to your liver and kidneys that is located just below the rib cage on the LEFT on the front slightly to the side. Make a 3 to 4 inch in diameter circle with the potato paste on the paper towel. I had a patient with Grave's disease who had extremely high thyroid hormones, over an immeasurable level, who could drop them down dramatically with this method in conjunction with a prescription.

Have a good night's sleep!

The color of the potato will have changed by the following morning. You will be amazed how toxic you are . . . There are so many different ways to detoxify your systems. Some chiropractors may use a detox machine like a foot bath, where the water color changes amazingly.

*Why Do I Have Thyroid Symptoms? When My Lab Tests Are Normal* by Dr. Datis Kharrazian DHSc, DC, MS is another interesting book to read for thyroid patients.

He is really good and has trained so many naturopathic doctors, chiropractors, and acupuncturists by providing the seminars. Although the products by Apex Energetic are very good, I think they have difficulty in reversing autoimmune thyroid conditions as Grave's disease and Hashimoto's disease unless patients follow a strict diet as far as I know. I could be wrong. I think he is getting close to burned out. Don't drain him so much. It happened to me in the past.

The website, www.brimhall.com, is also good for thyroid patients. Some Hashimoto's disease is reversed in conjunction with nutritional support and laser therapy.

Hashimoto's disease jumped up to five million from one million in the past ten years. It destroys thyroid tissue. Thyroid conditions are pandemic worldwide and are increasing among young generations as well. Patients with Hashimoto or low thyroid have difficulty in losing weight, constipation, sleep disturbance, feel cold, fatigue, and so forth. Hyperthyroid patients experience difficulty in gaining weight in spite of a good appetite, may experience diarrhea, feel hot, heat intolerance, rapid heart rate, sleep disturbance, fatigue, and so on. See your medical doctor first and check your thyroid function by blood test. If it does not show up on the blood test, consult with functional doctors if you have those symptoms. Know your body before it is too late.

**Coffee Enema**

Use a syringe to inject coffee into your rear end. Coffee is pure acid so that it will kill bacteria as well.

**Oil Pulling**

Put one teaspoon or tablespoonful of your favorite oil such as coconut oil or vegetable oil in your mouth and squish around for fifteen minutes. This is an Ayurveda method, the ancient remedy to drain your sinuses and take out pus and bacteria in your mouth.

Your teeth become brighter and smoother. I was amazed that my friend's husband got some infection in his mouth and had major swelling around his mouth. The swelling was gone after repeating this procedure a few times. Oral hygiene is very important.

You don't have to do everything I said here, you are the only person to prove it by trying the potato patch or other methods and see how you feel afterward. The good thing is, they are cheap and safe, the bad thing is, it requires work and patience to repeat.

Another cheap way to detoxify your liver and kidney function is to use Japanese yam cake. Both my mother and my mother-in-law had kidney failure. My mother went to kidney dialysis and passed away after three years of this treatment. My mother-in-law refused kidney dialysis and kidney transplant and went into hospice care. We got a phone call from our sister and found out she was critical. I packed up my suitcase with Japanese yam cakes and flew down to see her. I was shocked and expected she was dying in a few days. She was very conservative and did not want to try anything unusual, so I heated up the yam cake in boiling water for three to five minutes and wrapped it in a layered towel. I told her to lie down with this heat pack and apply it for thirty minutes. She repeated it several times on that day and I instructed my sister-in-law to apply the yam cake. She could get up on the following day and could walk around the house in a few days. Japanese yam cakes are less than $1 and you can reuse the yam cake for four or five times. Put it in a container, cover it up with water, and store in the refrigerator. I was amazed that she survived for one and a half year under hospice care. Acupuncturists would work on those cases as well to revitalize the organs when medications resulted in kidney or liver dysfunction, it just takes so long to revitalize the organs by acupuncture, combining the methods I described may speed up healing.

We, Asian people, believe foods have healing property so we eat yam cakes and taro potatoes. I heard a man who was diagnosed with kidney failure and was told that medical doctors could not do anything for his kidneys. He ate the yam cake every day for six months and found out his kidney function became normal.

Check out an Asian market and get a dark-gray colored one

in a plastic bag with water. It is about four inches x three inches, a rectangle shaped food also known as devil's tongue. The Japanese name for yam cake is konnyaku. One of my patients went to a Japanese grocery store and she was guided to the confectionary section. It's not a cake! Ask for the tofu section as yam cakes are usually located in that section. Sometimes, my husband screams when he finds something weird in the refrigerator.

Back Up! Back Up! Like your computer, save your organs.

**Bedtime**

Go to bed at 10:00 p.m. and sleep for eight hours. It is the ideal, based on the circadian rhythms as well as the biological clock, but it is hard to discipline . . . I wonder who follows this rule except for young kids. The United States also has a high incidence of insomnia.

Mothers with a baby who cries for milk in the middle of the night and people under so much stress cannot sleep well, and thyroid patients have problems sleeping. Frequent flyers who cross time zones may have problems adjusting the circadian rhythms due to jet lag for a while. My recommendation is to have carbohydrates for dinner such as pasta, grain, noodles, and so on and have a protein dish for breakfast and lunch. Some researchers recommend taking a nap during the day for one hour. I don't blame you if you do not follow this rule as I am not good at this rule, either.

**Drinking soda**

Regular soda contains a lot of sugar and diet soda contains aspartame that is a neurotoxin made from the same chemicals used in pesticides. There are not many differences in not gaining weight and it increases the risk of getting pancreatic cancer. Many of them contain caffeine to give you a high.

**Not only your diet, but also daily use items may induce cancer**

Detergent and laundry items, including stain removers and softeners, may induce cancer.

Chlorine affects motor nerves and is also documented to induce cancer.

The skin is the largest organ in our body. Frequent usage of the daily use items such as deodorant, need to be selected carefully and paid more attention.

Soap: bath soap, dish soap, hand soap, face soap, shampoo, conditioner may induce cancer.

Cosmetics: many of them are made from gasoline.

Skin care for sunlight. Sunscreen actually reacts to sun.

**Recommendations**

Use gloves for cleaning and minimize direct contact with strong cleaning products. We are living in such a toxic world. Some naturopathic doctors check out the skin care items, soaps, cosmetics and others. Naturopathic doctors can do so much with your conditions. I also like and trust the Life Extension medical doctors and much information is coming from medical journals not only by Life Extension, but also others. I recommend consulting with those doctors and other health care professionals.

**Muscle test**

Your body reacts with items by direct contact as all humans are electrical. This test requires two to three people. One person is a tester and checks the other person's original strength of his or her arm. (If a person has shoulder pain or elbow pain, use a different way described below to check the strength.) The person holds an item in his/her left arm or left hand and stretches out the other arm. (Keep in mind that a tester needs to use the same pressure and the person tested needs to keep his/her elbow straight.) Then the tester pushes down the stretched arm.

For those who have difficulty in testing, place the item over the person and touch the person. Use the same method described above as a surrogate test which requires an additional person. Some researchers concluded that surrogate testing is more accurate. This method is not a test for muscle strength so you may need to practice the amount of pressure to apply.

Usually it does not require so much force. Another modified way is to pull apart the fingers, usually I use the thumb and index finger, to form an O shape so it is called the O-ring test. This method could require a little more attention because the wrist position may change the strength. With either testing method, a positive means the stretched arm or testing fingers should be strong against the pressure and does not drop down or cannot be pulled apart that means your body accepts it. A negative means your arm drops down or your fingers are pulled apart that means that your body does not accept it.

I am amazed that so many supplements that my patients are taking are not the kinds their bodies need. If you want to use this method before you buy, you may want to do it at the natural food store to pick up the right kind. You can also do the same test to check any items, foods or drinks, daily use items and so on.

**Have fun!**

I list some of the articles from Life Extension on how to prevent and to back up other conditions.

**Cocoa May Help Diabetes, Heart Failure**
*United Press International*
03-05-12

Patients with advanced heart failure and Type 2 diabetes showed improvement after three months of consuming epicatechin-enriched cocoa, US researchers said.

Dr. Francisco J. Villarreal of University of California, San Diego, said epicatechin is a flavonoid found in dark chocolate.

The researchers examined five profoundly ill patients with major damage to skeletal muscle mitochondria—

structures responsible for most of the energy produced in cells. These "fuel cells" are dysfunctional as a result of both Type 2 diabetes and heart failure, leading to abnormalities in skeletal muscle, Villarreal said.

Patients with heart failure and diabetes experience abnormalities in both the heart and skeletal muscle that can result in impaired functional capacity. They often complain of shortness of breath, lack of energy, and have difficulty walking even short distances.

Trial participants consumed dark chocolate bars and a beverage with a total epicatechin content of approximately 100 milligram per day for three months. Biopsies of skeletal muscle were conducted before and after treatment.

After three months, the researchers looked at changes in mitochondria volume and the abundance of cristae, are internal compartments of mitochondria necessary for efficient function of the mitochondria.

"The cristae had been severely damaged and decreased in quantity in these patients," Villarreal said in a statement. "After three months, we saw recovery -- cristae numbers back toward normal levels, and increases in several molecular indicators involved in new mitochondria production."

The findings were published in the journal, *Clinical and Translational Science.*

Copyright United Press International 2012.

Articles featured in Life Extension Daily News are derived from a variety of news sources and are provided as a service by Life Extension. These articles, while of potential interest to readers of Life Extension Daily News, do not necessarily represent the opinions nor constitute the advice of Life Extension.

Some say eating apples, cinnamon, or drinking coffee may

reduce blood sugar. I would recommend that you work together with health care professionals, particularly if you have complications.

## Sleeping Pills 'Raise the Risk of Dying'
*The Herald*
02-28-12

Sleeping pills commonly prescribed in the UK may increase the risk of death more than four-fold, according to new research.

The higher the dose, the greater the risk of dying, while people on higher doses also had higher risks of cancer, experts found.

A wide range of drugs was analyzed for the study of more than 10,500 people taking sleeping pills.

They included drugs used in the UK, such as benzodiazepines (including temazepam and diazepam), non-benzodiazepines, barbiturates, and sedative antihistamines.

Around one-third of people in the UK are thought to have bouts of insomnia. It tends to be more common in women and older people.

Experts at the Jackson Hole Center for Preventive Medicine in Wyoming and the Scripps Clinic Viterbi Family Sleep Center in California, found people prescribed sleeping pills were 4.6 times more likely to die during a 2.5 year period compared to those not on the drugs.

Those taking four to eighteen pills a year had a 3.6 times higher risk of dying compared to non-users.

But the higher the dose, the greater the risk - with those taking 18 to 132 pills a year having a 4.4 times higher risk of dying, and people on more than 132 pills a year having a 5.3 times higher chance.

The researchers, writing in the journal, *BMJ Open*, concluded "Patients prescribed any hypnotic had substantially elevated hazards of dying." *BMJ Open* editor-in-chief, Dr. Trish Groves said, "These findings raise concerns about the safety of sleeping pills."

Articles featured in Life Extension Daily News are derived from a variety of news sources and are provided as a service by Life Extension. These articles, while of potential interest to readers of Life Extension Daily News, do not necessarily represent the opinions nor constitute the advice of Life Extension.

### Ask the Expert: Dr. Howard Kaufman on Aspirin and Cancer

Bonnie Miller Rubin
*Chicago Tribune*
03-28-12
March 28--According to studies published last week in *The Lancet*, taking a daily dose of aspirin can reduce the risk of cancer.

The new studies, led by Peter Rothwell of Britain's Oxford University, found that low-dose aspirin has a short-term benefit in preventing cancer and can reduce the risk of some cancers by as much as 50 percent.

For further clarification, we turned to Dr. Howard Kaufman, director of the Rush University Cancer Center at Rush University Medical Center. His primary research interest is melanoma and tumor immunotherapy, and he has more than 120 articles and other publications to his credit. Here's what he had to say about this cheap, over-the-counter pill that's in nearly everyone's medicine chest:

**Q.** What have we learned from these findings?
**A.** I think we've suspected aspirin had a beneficial role to play

in preventing cancer, and these two long-term studies go a long way in supporting that notion. Some studies in the United States haven't found this, but these recent studies are very well-designed and very compelling. A lot of us in the field are excited about the findings.

**Q.** How will this change things?
**A.** The good news: We have something that could help prevent cancer. But like all medications, there are side effects, such as stomach bleeding, peptic ulcers, and hemorrhagic stroke in the brain. So, we're not quite ready to prescribe this for everyone. We have to consider the cancer risk vs. the risk of stroke or a bleeding disorder.

**Q.** Did the studies find that an aspirin works on particular cancers?
**A.** The greatest effect was seen in colorectal cancer, but some effect was seen in many other types of cancer. This included some of the most common and serious cancers, such as lung, breast, and prostate cancers.

**Q.** So, who should take aspirin?
**A.** I think we can consider individuals with a high risk for or strong family history of colon cancer would be a good candidate . . . However, if a patient has a peptic ulcer or known bleeding problems, then the risks aren't worth the potential benefits.

**Q.** Can you explain how aspirin works in preventing cancer?
**A.** Although we do not fully understand the mechanism yet, there's been interesting research suggesting that aspirin may help prevent cancer by blocking chronic inflammation. When you cut yourself, your body uses a process called acute inflammation to heal and repair itself. But with cancer, the type

of inflammation is not completely "normal." We refer to this as chronic inflammation that continues without stopping. Aspirin may lower the rate of this chronic inflammation, and this may prevent the cancers from growing.

**Q.** In recent years, aspirin has been credited with reducing heart disease, asthma, and Parkinson's disease. How come people don't consider this a wonder drug?
**A.** It is remarkable. It has been difficult to fund research in cancer prevention -- and particularly with aspirin -- because prevention studies take a long time to complete, cost a lot of money to perform, and aspirin is a relatively inexpensive and widely available drug. Thus, there's not a lot of financial incentive to pursue this line of research.

**Q.** I know what to do to cut my chances of having a cardiac episode -- keep weight, blood pressure, and cholesterol under control, don't smoke, and exercise. What can we do to reduce the odds of a biopsy coming back positive?
**A.** First, you have to assess the risk, such as personal medical history, use of tobacco and alcohol and the presence of cancer in first-degree relatives . . . Then, a screening plan can be organized for an individual patient based on their risk . . . You should be having a conversation with your doctor, based on your health and family history.

brubin@tribune.com (c)2012 the Chicago Tribune Visit the Chicago Tribune at www.chicagotribune.com Distributed by MCT Information Services.

Articles featured in Life Extension Daily News are derived from a variety of news sources and are provided as a service by Life

Extension. These articles, while of potential interest to readers of Life Extension Daily News, do not necessarily represent the opinions nor constitute the advice of Life Extension.

## Life Extension Update

Some patients may want to take aspirin to prevent cancer, but I list the other alternative ways to prevent cancers. Some people who have thin capillaries may bleed more by taking aspirin. I recommend knowing your body and teaming up with your doctors.

Concerning the troubles on sleep, you may have high adrenal stress or thyroid conditions. People under so much stress these days have trouble sleeping and thyroid conditions are rapidly increasing worldwide. Even young children and teenagers can get thyroid conditions. Blood tests are not quite sensitive enough to detect thyroid conditions. Medical doctors do not check out adrenal function oftentimes for thyroid patients.

Thyroid conditions are also linked with the hypothalamus, pituitary gland and adrenal glands. Supporting adrenal glands is another option for better sleep. I would say any endocrine problems are closely related to stress to the digestive system.

The majority of my patients who are under high stress have both high adrenal stress and digestive stress. You may want to check out your caffeine consumption and the timing you drink as well. Eat turkey or chicken, which are high in tryptophan, to relax you for dinner. Avoid any stimulating activities before bedtime and deep breathing on your bed also helps you to fall asleep.

My recommendation for adrenal stress is Adrenal complex by Transformation.

You may want to consult with your chiropractor or naturopathic doctor who has contracts with Transformation or they may have different kinds of supplements to support the adrenal glands.

A bath soak at night is also relaxing and you can enjoy it with different kinds of bath salts.

Another way to relax is to use essential oils as the nose is also close to the brain; you can sniff, put the oil in the water to bathe and wear it. I put essential oils to shine under my patients' noses. Sometimes, people are not aware that they don't smell equally. Knowing how your body is functioning is important.

The website, www.youngliving.com, is good for essential oil products or check out natural food stores or shops for body care products.

Essential oils also have more healing power for various conditions and it is interesting to check out the research by this company.

## Higher Lutein and Zeaxanthin Levels May Help Protect Against Cataracts

**Tuesday, March 13, 2012.** In an article published in advance of print in the *British Journal of Nutrition*, Jouni Karppi and Sudhir Kurl at the University of Eastern Finland in Kuopio and Jari Laukkanen of Lapland Central Hospital in Rovaniemi, Finland report that increased plasma levels of the carotenoids lutein and zeaxanthin are associated with a lower risk of cataract in older men and women. Lutein and zeaxanthin's protective effect against another eye disease--age-related macular degeneration—is well known, however their effects in other eye conditions have been less well explored.

"Reactive oxygen species can damage lens proteins and fiber cell membranes, leading to cataract formation," the authors write. "Lutein and zeaxanthin are the most abundant carotenoids that accumulate in the lens of the eye, where they possibly filter phototoxic blue light and neutralize reactive oxygen species."

The current study included 1,130 men and 559 women who enrolled in the Kuopio Ischemic Heart Disease Risk Factor Study from 1998-2001. Blood plasma samples collected between 2005 and 2008 were analyzed for alpha tocopherol, vitamin A, and carotenoids.

From the beginning of the current investigation through 2008, 113 cataracts were diagnosed, including 108 nuclear cataracts (the most common cataract type, believed to be caused in part by free radical damage), resulting in a four year nuclear cataract incidence of 6.4 percent. Among subjects whose lutein levels were among the top one-third of participants, there was a 42 percent lower risk of being diagnosed with nuclear cataract, and for those whose zeaxanthin levels were among the top third, the risk was 41 percent lower compared to subjects whose plasma levels were in the lowest third.

While three cross-sectional studies have found a lower risk of nuclear cataract or their progression in association with higher serum levels or dietary intake of lutein and zeaxanthin, the current study's authors note that a recent FDA review concluded that there was no credible evidence to support a protective effect for lutein or zeaxanthin on cataract risk. However, Dr. Karppi and colleagues remark that there are factors that could explain previous inconsistent study results.

"We observed that high concentrations of lutein and zeaxanthin were associated with a reduced risk of nuclear cataract in elderly subjects," they conclude. "There may be other protective factors

of the diet (e.g. synergism of carotenoids with vitamin C or other antioxidants) that may partly explain the observed results."

An article published online on December 8, 2011 in the journal, *Free Radical Biology and Medicine,* shows a protective effect for grapes and lutein against the development of age-related macular degeneration (AMD) in a mouse model of the disease.

In their introduction to the article, Silvia Finnemann, PhD of Fordham University's Department of Biological Sciences and her associates explain that oxidative damage and pro-oxidant lysosomal lipofuscin accumulate in the aging human eye, which causes a decline in function of the retinal pigment epithelium: the support cells for the retina's photoreceptors. The resulting dysfunction and destruction of these cells, in turn, contributes to the development of age-related macular degeneration.

For their study, Dr Finnemann's team administered diets that provided natural antioxidants, grapes or marigold extract containing the macular pigments lutein/zeaxanthin to mice bred to have increased blood vessel formation (which occurs in macular degeneration). While lutein and zeaxanthin proved to be protective to the eye, grapes showed the greatest benefit, with both compounds resulting in reduced lipofuscin accumulation and age related rod and cone photoreceptor dysfunction, prevention of blindness, and other positive outcomes. The antioxidant properties of compounds that occur in grapes are believed to be the protective mechanism observed in the current research.

"The protective effect of the grapes in this study was remarkable, offering a benefit for vision at old age even if grapes were consumed only at young age," Dr Finnemann stated. "A lifelong diet enriched in natural antioxidants, such as those in grapes, appears to be directly beneficial for retinal pigment epithelium, and retinal health and function."

### Artificial Hip Brings Only Pain
James Walsh, Star Tribune, Minneapolis
*Knight Ridder/Tribune Business News*
03-12-12

**March 12**--Terri Wagner-Morley was so hopeful about her new right hip.

It would ease her chronic arthritis pain, allow her to exercise, even help her lose a little weight. She had a DePuy metal-on-metal ASR hip implanted in 2008 and, at first, it worked just like she'd hoped.

"It felt great," she said. "I could move again." Her weight dropped from 219 pounds to 165 in a year.

Then she began feeling a "pop" in the hip. The pop turned to pain, making it hurt to move. By late 2009, she'd regained all the weight. Wagner-Morley's hip had failed years before it was supposed to.

Her case, like thousands of others in the United States, has contributed to growing concerns about possible damage from metal-on-metal hips. Reported problems include loosening of the hip, inflammation in the tissues around the hip, dislocation, and, in some cases, increased metal particles in the bloodstream. The US Food and Drug Administration has ordered manufacturers to further study the safety of metal-on-metal hips. Thousands of lawsuits have been filed.

There are various types of metal-on-metal hips, many showing no problems whatsoever. Still, some doctors are moving away from metal-on-metal hips, once seen as potentially more resistant to wear and tear than artificial hips made from other materials. Minnesota's renowned Mayo Clinic has dramatically curtailed its use of the metal devices.

Dr. David Lewallen, a Mayo orthopedic surgeon, said

more data on metal-on-metal hips needs to be gathered, saying they remain a viable option for some patients. But he acknowledged the array of concerns. "That continues to be a mystery, what is going on in these patients," he said. "And that continues to be the ongoing mystery and the focus of investigation and work now."

Dr. Alan Knopf, an orthopedic surgeon who teaches at UCLA and USC, went a step further. "This metal-on-metal concept . . . has lost enthusiasm in the medical community," he said.

A better hip?

Introduced in the late 1960s, modern hip replacement is a success story, said Dr. Joshua Jacobs, a professor and chairman of Orthopedic Surgery at Rush University Medical Center in Chicago.

It has allowed people who had been condemned to a life of pain, to "return to normal lives with high levels of function." About 400,000 people in the United States have hip replacement surgery each year, Jacobs said. While total dollar amounts are difficult to obtain, Medicare alone spends about $20 billion a year on implantable medical devices. Artificial hips make up a healthy portion of that total.

Despite their overwhelming success, Jacobs said, most artificial hips have a realistic survival of ten to fifteen years. But as surgeons implant hips into younger and more-active people, they continue searching for hips that last longer.

Jacobs said three total hip systems have been most common: Hips with a ceramic-coated ball in a ceramic cup, hips with a metal ball in a metal cup and hips with a metal ball fit into a polyethylene cup.

"In 2012, we still are aware that the implants we are putting in today might not last for as long as our patients need them," said Jacobs, who is a vice president for the American Academy of

Orthopedic Surgeons. "There is always a search for our ultimate desire, which would be the lifetime total hip replacement. We're not there yet."

DePuy voluntarily recalled its ASR hip in August 2010 and has recommended that all patients have their hip evaluated by their doctor. It has set up a help line and reimbursement program. DePuy issued its recall after receiving data from the United Kingdom showing that 13 percent of its ASR metal-on-metal hips needed replacement within five years.

For DePuy's ASR Hip Resurfacing System, that "revision rate" was 12 percent. Mindy Tinsley, a DePuy spokeswoman, said 37,000 ASR hips were implanted in the United States. Tinsley said she does not know how many of those hips were implanted in Minnesota.

Even though "the majority of patients with metal-on-metal hips are doing well," Jacobs said concerns about those hips have led surgeons to look to other materials. Metal-on-metal hips once were used in about one-third of all total hip procedures, he said. Now, they make up less than 5 percent.

At Mayo, Lewallen said, doctors are looking at a metal-on-plastic hip that uses a new, harder plastic. So far, he said, the results have been promising.

"There is no perfect technology," Lewallen said. "It is a matter of weighing the advantages, or disadvantages, of a particular device."

Still waiting . . .

An infection has kept doctors from replacing Wagner-Morley's DePuy hip, which they removed on Dec. 29. She also faces continued uncertainty about when her life will return to some kind of normal.

She is the mother of twin daughters in college and a grown son. She is living at a friend's townhouse in Rosemount. Spacers fill the place where her hip should be. She cannot walk, she cannot work. For a time, her kidneys and her liver failed.

Wagner-Morley said she just wants to get her life back.

"I'm just so happy I am alive," she said. "But it's frustrating as heck."

Broadspire, the company handling claims of DePuy patients, has indicated they will pay for Wagner-Morley's new surgery, said her attorney, Mark Karney. Still, some type of class-action lawsuit is expected, he said.

"It's turned her life upside down," he said. "All of this stuff is, in my opinion, a direct result of a defective hip."

James Walsh --612-673-7428 (c) 2012 the Star Tribune (Minneapolis) Visit the Star Tribune (Minneapolis) at www. startribune.com Distributed by MCT Information Services Swiss:SYST.

Articles featured in Life Extension Daily News are derived from a variety of news sources and are provided as a service by Life Extension. These articles, while of potential interest to readers of Life Extension Daily News, do not necessarily represent the opinions nor constitute the advice of Life Extension.

**The Good News is Your Terminal Disease Was a Misdiagnosis-** The Bad News is You're Going to Die From it; Dr. Jeffery Stuart and Sally Pacholok RN Speak Out on Hidden Health Epidemic

*PrimeNewswire*

02-22-12

**DETROIT, Feb. 22, 2012** (GLOBE NEWSWIRE) -- An

epidemic of misdiagnoses are killing and crippling people, according to physician Jeffery Stuart and Sally Pacholok, RN, mostly because the real, easily correctable problem imitates a variety of terminal diseases, then turns lethal itself when ignored: vitamin B-12 deficiency.

Millions of people needlessly suffer and even die from this common vitamin deficiency. Doctors mistakenly think their patients have multiple sclerosis, Alzheimer's, autism, anemia, depression, chronic fatigue, or some other disease or condition mimicked by B-12 deficiency.

"The shame is that the problem is easy to spot, easy to treat, easy to cure, and costs very little money," say Stuart and Pacholok, co-authors of the only book on the subject. "But that's only if your doctor diagnoses you before it's too late. Unfortunately, that frequently doesn't happen."

Their message is catching on. Dr. Oz just did an entire show on B-12 this January, 2012.

Stuart and Pacholok say the entire health crisis (and the related financial burden from expensive treatments for misdiagnosed disease as well as malpractice lawsuits) could be solved with a simple change in the standard of care that would encourage health care professionals to test for B-12 deficiency whenever people show symptoms of the diseases it mimics.

"If insurance companies and our government knew how much money they were needlessly spending they would be on board immediately," Pacholok says. "Standardized testing and treatment of people found to be deficient, as well as those who are symptomatic and in the gray zone (B-12 levels between 200-450pg/ml, considered normal by many doctors), would save them billions of dollars."

Pacholok, a leading authority on B-12 deficiency, warns that if you are B-12 deficient, standard multivitamin pills won't help.

The reason? Most people are deficient because their digestive systems do not effectively absorb the vitamin.

"If you're deficient, swallowing a multivitamin is like adding a teaspoon of water to an empty swimming pool," Pacholok says.

The preferred way to take an oral vitamin B-12 supplement, Pacholok says, is by sublingual or micro-lingual absorption, where the vitamin dissolves under the tongue and directly enters the bloodstream. Some patients, however, may still require B-12 injections.

Available for Interview: Pacholok has done dozens of TV, radio, and print interviews including CNN Headline News and Redbook. She is co-author of the newly released second edition, *Could It Be B-12? An Epidemic of Misdiagnoses,* Quill Driver Books, (2nd Ed. 2011) (1st Ed. 2005).

Contact: Chris Kelley, publicist, at 406-333-9999 or chris@ polestarcom.com.

A file archive accompanying this release is available at http:// media.globenewswire.com/cache/19143/file/12626.jpg

This news release was distributed by GlobeNewswire, www. globenewswire.com Copyright PrimeNewswire 2012.

Articles featured in Life Extension Daily News are derived from a variety of news sources and are provided as a service by Life Extension. These articles, while of potential interest to readers of Life Extension Daily News, do not necessarily represent the opinions nor constitute the advice of Life Extension.

**Vitamin D Helps Relieve Menstrual Symptoms**

**Friday, March 2, 2012.** A research letter published in the

February 27, 2012 issue of the American Medical Association journal, *Archives of Internal Medicine,* reported the results of a study of women with primary dysmenorrhea that found that a single high dose of oral vitamin D3 reduced pain over a two month period. Dysmenorrhea is characterized by painful

uterine cramping that is often accompanied by nausea, vomiting, diarrhea, and other symptoms. The condition affects at least half of premenopausal girls and women, and can have a major impact on work and school attendance and performance.

Excessive uterine production of hormone-like substances known as prostaglandins is a major cause of dysmenorrhea, which is commonly treated with nonsteroidal anti-inflammatory drugs.

For the current trial, Antonio Lasco, MD, Antonino Catalano, MD and Salvatore Benvenga, MD of the University of Messina in Italy enrolled forty women between the ages of eighteen and forty who reported at least four painful periods over the previous six months and whose serum 25-hydroxyvitamin D levels were lower than forty-five nanograms per milliliter. Twenty participants were administered 300,000 international units (IU) vitamin D3 five days before the beginning of their next menstrual cycle, while the remainder received a placebo. Pain symptoms were scored before treatment and at one and two months.

A correlation was observed at the beginning of the study between increased pain scores and reduced serum vitamin D levels. Women who received vitamin D reported a significant reduction in pain over two months compared to the placebo group. While 40 percent of subjects who received a placebo took nonsteroidal anti-inflammatory drugs for pain at least once over the course of the trial, none who received vitamin D reported needing the drugs. The greatest benefits were observed among those reporting the highest level of pain at the beginning of the study. The authors explain that vitamin D decreases proinflammatory cytokines and regulates the expression of genes involved in the prostaglandin pathway, reducing prostaglandin activity.

In an invited commentary in the journal, Elizabeth R. Bertone-Johnson, DSc and JoAnn E. Manson, MD note that it is important to determine how long a reduction in pain in association with a single dose of vitamin D would last. They note that "If 300,000 IU is required every two months, this would equate to approximately 5000 IU per day, considerably higher than the tolerable upper intake level set by the Institute of Medicine of 4000 IU/day."

"If these findings are confirmed in future randomized trials, vitamin D supplementation may become an important new treatment option for women who experience menstrual pain disorders" they conclude.

Recommendation

Get a sun bath for fifteen minutes a day. These days Vitamin D is a hot item! According to the oncologist, Dr. David B Agus, M.D. vitamin D prevents certain cancers, autoimmune diseases, flu, and so many other conditions.

Google is convenient to find out so many things. Vitamin D itself has over two million articles. Don't drive yourself and your doctor crazy! Control is the key.

# PLASTIC, PLASTIC, PLASTICITY

Plastic surgery changes appearance. I was hooked on a Korean soap opera at one period of time and watched over and over, crying at the sad love stories. One day, I realized these beautiful Korean actresses had plastic surgeries. Then I noticed that their eyes did not move in certain directions so that I started to analyze which eye muscles were damaged as I got involved in neurology classes then. So much for crying that has a good therapeutic effect. Laughing is another therapeutic effect, if you are depressive, I recommend watching really funny movies. Plastic surgery may give you a beautiful appearance for a while, but it does not to give you permanent beauty. It often requires additional surgery to keep up its features. Our skin changes by aging, boobs hang down, buttocks sag down, gravity is always the winner in the long term. Botox is used to block out the neurosynaptic junction so that some patients become paralyzed, which has brought major lawsuits. Is it worth it to lose some normal functions? Everyone has different sets of values. How much do you want to spend and how much risk do you want to take? It's all your choice. Well, I feel so sorry for Michael Jackson as he needed such strong pain killers at the end of his life.

**Plastic bottles, bags, and containers** change the content. If you sip water from a plastic bottle, finish drinking it as soon as possible, the bacteria from your mouth spreads and grows in the bottle. Organic foods need to be wrapped in a paper bag;

otherwise, it becomes nonorganic. Plastic shower heads grow bacteria/virus that may cause infections or TB (Tuberculosis).

**Recommendation:Replace with a metal shower head.**

Plasticity is a neurological terminology that means neurons and pathways change due to excitability. There is considerable evidence for plasticity at chemical synapses that would result in physiological and anatomical changes and even creates new growth.

Everything changes, nothing stays the same. You can make changes to get better. Make small changes little by little, it may take a while to get used to and to make it as a good habit. We may quit good habits, but you can always go back to a good habit. Continuation, little by little, makes a big difference in the long term. If you force it, you feel uncomfortable like a tight bra or blue jeans to squeeze out your fat. People sometimes force themselves to make it happen. "I can do it!" or "You can do it!" Typical man's mentality . . . I know you can. It will make you feel uncomfortable, exhausted, you may get hurt by forcing it and often, it does not last long. For instance, biking, weight training, any physical activities using joint motion will cause some risks of harm unless you stretch out the muscles in the long term. What I am saying here is not that exercises are harmful, but it can be harmful without knowing how your body functions and depending on the kinds and depending how you do it. Excess is similar to insufficiency and can be harmful. We need both muscle contraction and stretching and how to keep up the maintenance in the long term. The majority of patients don't really feel the minor changes, how the joints are formed, and how to stretch the muscles well. A woman went to a gym and started on the tread mill. She did not know that her ankles and knees were unstable so that she ended up with knee surgery. Even if you think exercise is good for you, forcing it affects the weakened areas. The rule of thumb is to stop when you feel uncomfortable or pain. It is the same as mental or emotional stress, people go crazy on exercise, shopping, gambling until they break down their body or finances. As I said earlier, it's all good and bad, it all depends on which aspect you focus on. Particularly, emotionally linked habits are hard to break. A *Reader's Digest's* article talks about forty-one things that doctors never tell their patients. One of them was that the doctor says "Lose twenty pounds." He really means lose fifty pounds! Usually, people have sugar or caffeine or smoke a cigarette in the morning and afternoon to boost their energy. All sorts of activities we do, including work can be addictive. Negativity itself does not have any negativity. As we deny negativity, we create negativity. If nobody enjoys it, it does not exist. Everything is enjoyable for those who choose. Some people, particularly women, crave chocolate in the afternoon or after the meal. Dark chocolate has high antioxidants, more than blueberries; however, it is usually added up with other junk in dark chocolates. That's the problem. The majority of food has both good and bad effects and we cannot eliminate all the risk factors that cause fatal diseases. I would say control is the major issue. Life itself has both good and bad aspects. You may have a bad day or bad time, sometimes it is good. As we have both, we can enjoy our life. Life is a tragedy for some people and life is a comedy for those who enjoy it. Similar to the small stain on a white shirt, it bothers you when you focus on the stain; it does not bother you unless you look at it. The same is true inside your body. Everybody has two eyes, one mouth, one nose, and two ears when we look at a face. Everyone has two lungs, one heart, one stomach, and so forth. All human beings have the same structure under their skin anatomically. Do you remember the physiology that I explained to you briefly earlier? My question is, who eats the same foods for their entire life? Who has the same experiences like you do? Who has the same orientation that you have? Nobody! All those factors you went through in your life formed you as a person, a very unique individual like everyone else. It is not the question of good or bad or superior or inferior. It is just different! Inside of you, you are unique. Anatomically, there is not much difference between men and women except for the reproductive organs. Some males seem to have their second brain in their sexual organ. As a matter of fact, I found out the male sexual organ is innervated by the same nerve to innervate the colon. It makes sense! Emotionality exceeds intellect oftentimes. Former Presidents John F. Kennedy and Bill Clinton and Tiger Woods are good examples. People under so much stress do crazy things. Sexuality is also bad and good, it all depends on how you control yourself. Some of them harass, molest, and rape in the worst case. If you force it, it is a major problem and a crime. The emotional trauma affects the physical body as well as the mentality and one incidence may trash the person's whole life. As long as they agree and use control, including the risk of pregnancy, it is not my business. I saw a banner on a plane saying, "Can't wait wearing it! Trojan." One of my friends who is a herbalist and acupuncturist told me she was on birth control pills that resulted in different problems and cost her so much. Mesh also became a big lawsuit. Many drugs including prescriptions are involved in lawsuits and some law firms are encouraging the lawsuits. Even over-the-counter pills for the common cold were documented to cause internal bleeding in the brain after ingestion for three days in a row. I saw the same emails after three years and was shocked those pills were still on the market! The question is, who prescribes and who agrees to take it? The FDA is supposed to control the regulations for prescriptions and over-the-counter pills, isn't it?

One of my patients who was around sixty went to see her OB/GYN doctor and was told that she needs to have orgasms sixteen times every day. I told her, "If you really love your husband, you may want to think about getting a toy rather than getting Viagra." Our bodies don't like anything artificial and usually counteract in a period of time. When we are young, we can do more physical activities and we do less physical as we age. Aging sucks! We cannot see small letters, we cannot hear you well. It hurts! On the other hand, aging is also a process on how to learn to take care of ourselves better. Also aging creates a miracle by our accumulated knowledge and experiences. I did not to expect to write a book, particularly in my second language when I was young. It's a miracle! It all depends on what we focus on and how we use it.

Some doctors who work hard to help their patients by using different approaches may lose their license unless they follow the regulations, even if their patients are happy with the results. Concerning the three major treatments for cancer, on his website, Dr. Coldwell, MD stated that chemotherapy is to poison the body, radiation therapy is to burn the body, and surgery is to chop up the body. He also stated that medicine should be affordable for each individual. He recommends an organic food diet, detoxification, and supports more natural approaches. I don't know who set up the five year survival rate and who can guarantee a person's life. Some cancer survivors may change their lifestyles and diet completely and survive much longer. Some patients stay the same way they were after therapy and get recurrent cancer after five years or so. Many of the patients who went through those procedures do not wish to go back to the same procedures. Some patients who went through surgery for colon cancer may lose their sensations for bowel movements after the surgery. Many patients who went through chemotherapy lose their hair and suffer from the side effects of the medication or may develop neuropathy. Everyone is so different due to their own genetic factors, their diet, environmental factors, mental and emotional stress, and so forth. It is very hard to say which medicine will work. It is a struggle for both doctors and patients. Suzanne Somers, the actress who is a breast cancer survivor and had stem cell implant in Europe, is a good example. The oncologist, David B. Agus, MD, stated in his audio book, *The End of Illness*, "The patient needs to take risks." That is very true; but, the question is, how much risk can a patient take and how much function does a patient lose? Isn't there any low risk cancer care? I also suppose the regulations may stop the doctors from performing other different methods so as not to lose their licenses. We, health care professionals, are afraid of losing our license to practice, not to violate the regulations, patient's lawsuits, and so on. Even though the majority of the patients are happy with the results, some doctors lost their license because of regulations or politics. In the book, *Sanctuary*, the doctor created a machine to measure the risk factors of the cancer or other diseases by application of electric current on the meridian points. Based on the findings, he prescribed tinctures to reverse the frequency. The cancer patient who lost her hair could recover from the cancer. I think he lost his license and some chiropractors have lost their licenses in the past even though the majority of their patients were happy with the results. I believe the majority of people need affordable insurance and medicine should not be expensive, but within an affordable range. Some of the oncologists may believe those procedures would cure the cancer, some of them may suspect what they are doing, and some of them are doing it because they learned that is the right way to do it without thinking, or some of them are doing it for more money linked with pharmaceutical companies. As I mentioned earlier, we all adapt to situations to fit in. Even if we feel uncomfortable in the beginning, we will get used to the changes. It will work in both good and bad ways. Once we get used to things, we often compromise unless a major event would happen for the changes. For instance, Medicare only allows chiropractors to adjust the spine only. It does not allow chiropractors to adjust their arms or legs. The majority of senior people become inactive and hit their knees or hips by falling or injuring their shoulders. Those are common complaints among senior patients; but, Medicare does not allow chiropractors to adjust their shoulders, knees, or wrists. Not only chiropractors, but also medical doctors are not reimbursed for the care so that many doctors refuse seeing those patients as a result. They are talking about cutting the budget on Medicare patients, more now. Politics always stinks.

It all depends on each practitioner's ethics, belief system, and passion to help patients; yet, losing your license or lawsuits are major factors in preventing doctors from providing adequate or a different approach to minimize the risk for patients. Malpractice insurance companies provide some information about the lawsuit cases. One of the lawsuits occurred against a chiropractor who performed a tail bone adjustment. He explained to the patient what he was going to do and had his assistant in the room. There is a procedure to correct tailbone adjustment by inserting the finger from the rectum to correct the tailbone position. The patient sued because she felt it was like a sexual assault in spite of her agreement. We, American people, threaten each other through lawsuits and create vicious cycles. There are not so many strict regulations in my home country to practice medicine; it is not a huge problem as far as I know. There are, of course, some malpractice cases reported in the newspapers and TV news. In China, a patient has a choice to have open heart surgery with or without anesthesia. We have a choice to use acupuncture instead of anesthesia. It is a patient's choice. We are open to many different approaches as long as doctors and the practitioners work on the premise of medicine working together. The major issue is to protect and to provide patients' necessary care under their specialty at affordable rate. I don't think it is a big problem to provide patient's needs if it works.

The Japanese internist, Dr. Kimihiko Okazaki created a tincture to reverse cancers and wrote a book, *Goodbye Incurable Diseases.* Japanese Nobel prize winner, Koichi Tanaka, who found the protein binding factor from waste material by accident, got involved in medicine these days.

The protein binding factors are the key to detect cancers so they created blood screening tests for various cancers. The blood test indicates various cancer risk factors in three zones, low risk, medium risk, or high risk on various cancers so that a doctor and a patient would get some ideas about the cancer risks. Why not import those new findings and create a new regulation by oncologists? Providing the blood screen tests by medical doctors and getting the training by the internist in Japan would be better for the patients and doctors to minimize the lawsuits. I don't blame oncologists who are afraid of losing their license; yet, regulations should change, otherwise medical fees will be huge for this cancer rate soon and more people may end up with personal bankruptcy, or people may just die without adequate medical care and oncologists may not be reimbursed by insurance companies and cancer hospitals are closing down. How can regular people pay $1000 for chemotherapy each time or more without insurance, sometimes procedures combined with chemotherapy can go over $9,000 for one chemotherapy session or more, which usually people will go through multiple times. Some patients die from the chemotherapy itself; there is no guarantee even though oncologists and surgeons work hard. Many insurance companies refuse to pay for those traditional cancer treatments, also. Concerning the side effects of chemotherapy and radiation therapy, I don't really want to pursue those medical interventions; rather, I prefer to work on preventative remedies. How can people afford those outrageous amounts of charges while people have squeezed budgets or have great trouble paying the premium? No wonder some American people become greedy and have so many lawsuits because there is not much support or security for regular workers. Notification of cancer itself is a death sentence for the majority of people, particularly young people. It is very frightening and I don't know how insurance companies will handle those medical charges as well for cancer patients in the near future. We need to make changes to stop this vicious cycle and we need to create different ways. What I observe is the higher the risk of the procedure, the higher the medical fee. Because we doctors are afraid of patients lawsuits and we need to pay a lot for malpractice insurance. What is this Obamacare? What happened after George Bush, Sr. and Jr.? Medicine should be affordable, reasonable, and everyone should be covered. We really need a major change.

Politics always stinks!

# CHIROPRACTIC WORKS

D. D. Palmer is the founder of chiropractic medicine and proclaimed chiropractic as a new procedure in 1895 after he corrected a patient with a hearing impairment by a neck adjustment. *Chiro* means hand in Greek so that chiropractic means that practice by hands. I believe everyone has healing hands as we apply our hand wherever it hurts as the primitive response and it eases the pain oftentimes. His son, B. J. Palmer, founded a chiropractic school in Iowa and taught the technique called HIO (hole in one) upper cervical technique. He adjusted only the highest segment of a spine in the neck, just below the skull. The segment is also known as atlas, that is the closest segment to the brain so that people experience a "miracle," oftentimes. The philosophy of the technique is the highest segment of a spine alignment will correct the entire spine as the spine hangs down from the top segment and the rest of the spine aligns following the top segment position. The major concept of chiropractic is that a misaligned spine, called subluxation, results in not only back or neck pain, but also various diseases or conditions. The nerve interference, pinched nerve, kinked nerve, whatever you call it, results in pain, tingling, numbness, or dysfunction in the arms, legs, and organ systems. As you know that our brain controls our body, the nervous system is the major control center. Dr. DeJarnette created another technique called SOT (sacro-occipital technique) about seventy-five years ago. It utilizes the blocks, which are wedge-shape tools, to correct pelvic torsion.

The philosophy of the technique is that the sacrum, (the upside-down triangle-shape bone at the center of the pelvis just above your tailbone) and the occiput (one of the cranial bones located at the back of your head) create a pumping mechanism to circulate CSF (cerebrospinal fluid). The spine sits on top of the sacrum so that we believe we need to correct the sacrum position along with occipital and cranial bone alignment. Patients lie on the blocks so that the patient's own body weight and breathing do the adjustment without force. Dr. De Jarnette was also an osteopathic doctor so that he modified and created the cranial procedures specific to chiropractors. Dr. De Jarnette teamed up with dentists and medical doctors to help patients. Dr. M.L. Rees studied under Dr. De Jarnette and created his own technique called STO (soft tissue orthopedic). Both of them created so many miracles such as a patient who was dying recovered by Dr. De Jernette's adjustment and the patient's face was not identifiable after a one-year treatment. I heard a patient with Down's syndrome had characteristic features and SOT cranial work correction changed the characteristic feature; however, I don't know if it would change the chromosome of DNA that results in Down's syndrome. Activation of the brain results in immediate early gene response according to the Nobel Prize winner. I suppose it is possible. Chiropractic care activates the nervous system. Back to the track! Dr. M. L. Rees was removing tumors, rebuilding bones in one to three adjustments, and created many procedures to reverse difficult conditions such as neurological conditions, autoimmune conditions, and so forth at his late stage of practice. Patients were flying into their offices from all over the world. I believe those doctors were a legend in chiropractic history. Then, those techniques were modified and diverged into over three hundred chiropractic techniques in use now. Dr. De Jarnette and Dr. Rees passed away in 1992. Dr. Carrick could be one of the legend doctors in chiropractic history in the future. He is still alive and active. Wakening up the vegetable state of the patients is a very remarkable way to give a life back to the patient. As far as I observed, not so many chiropractors, including myself, are not at these legend doctors levels, yet. You can still get so much benefit from the followers and many chiropractic techniques came from HIO, SOT, and STO. Among those chiropractic techniques, there are two mainstream techniques; one is called "straight chiropractors" who practice only osseous adjustment, who are more focused on correcting the spinal alignment. They usually apply force to manipulate the misaligned joints and their major techniques are Diversify and Gonstead. The majority of people have images that the popping or cracking of the neck and back is chiropractic. Those are this type of adjustment and is similar to cracking knuckles because misaligned joints contain carbon dioxide in the joint capsule. When you open a carbonated drink bottle, it creates the popping sound; many of your joints are like that. The other stream is chiropractors who combine different techniques, not necessarily forceful adjustment, but also very gentle techniques in conjunction with physical therapy and nutrition, a so called "mixture."

The Diversify technique is the most common technique used among chiropractors because it is the standard technique taught at chiropractic schools and national board exams these days. Each chiropractic school, however, has a different philosophy and each state has different regulations concerning the practice of chiropractic. Current school curriculum to become a chiropractor is the equivalent training to becoming a medical doctor. We just have a different philosophy about the body. We believe everybody has a natural healing ability, or so called innate intelligence. All animals and humans have this natural healing power; however, our body accumulates various stresses to our bodies and deteriorates by aging.

I practiced the Diversify technique for one year or so

after I started my practice and I worked hard on each patient to relieve their pain, along with physical therapy and massage that I learned at chiropractic school. I shared the office space with another chiropractor who practiced the Gonstead technique and the Thompson technique in which we use drop tables to adjust the spine with a force; but, it does not crack your spine most of the time. I found my patients came back with the same complaints and the same pain intensity oftentimes. I thought I may not have good adjustment skills around that time and started to take seminars for different chiropractic techniques, Activator (we use a spring utilized adjustment tool to adjust the spine and extremities with a minimum of force), TBM (total body modification) where they utilize the reflex points to adjust the spine with a spring utilized adjustment tool and has allergy desensitization and so many different protocols for various conditions as well. I have a friend who is a psychotherapist who referred me a three-year-old boy with pervasive learning disorder. He had a hearing test by an EENT specialist and found out his hearing was fine. I did different functional hearing tests by TBM on him that indicated the boy had a hearing problem so that I adjusted his atlas with the Activator gun. After the first visits, his pronunciation became clearer and the boy quit the care after two visits and found out he could enroll to a regular class later. I continued to take seminars, AK (applied kinesiology) that involves meridian points in conjunction with nutrition. I also took various nutrition seminars by different vitamin companies. Around that time, the senior doctor asked me to take care of his patients while he was on vacation. I agreed and took care of his patients. The majority of his patients told me I did a really good job and some of them requested to see me. Now, I had a major problem and I was kicked out from his office.

I found a different office to share shortly after so that I started practicing again and learned more on nutrition, more on SOT and STO. I got involved in the chiropractic neurology diplomat course later and am still learning more. I realized I went backwards because TBM is coming from AK and AK is coming from SOT and STO. What I learned was just modified and simplified SOT and STO. There are much more in the original work. Those techniques are more diverged techniques such as biophysics, Nucca (modified HIO), neuro emotional technique (NET) network (modified advance STO), DNFT (directional non forceful technique), BEST, Logan basic and so on, and those techniques are gentle in comparison to straight chiropractors. Chiropractors are very unique in combining different techniques, some of them use magnets or gemstones, and I realized that the concepts originated in Dr. M. L. Rees's early work for his energy work. The majority of chiropractors work in conjunction with physical therapy and many chiropractors started using cold laser therapy that is a relatively new wave. I was amazed that a frozen shoulder patient (cannot raise his or her arm above shoulder level) could raise his/her arm in one to two visits with laser therapy. The FDA approved cold laser therapy because a minor fracture can be healed in a week by cold laser therapy. We adjust joints, organs, and nerves to maintain its function. I believe the function of the body is the major factor on health.

What I understand about traditional medicine is that it is more focused on chemical balances. Prescription and over-the-counter pills mask the symptoms, so it is also called allopathic medicine. Concerning our body as a whole, we all need good chemical balance, structural balance, and emotional balance. All three factors interact with each other as we are emotionally driven living entities. Emotional stress affects chemical interactions in the body because adrenalin and cortisol secreted from the adrenal glands affect organs as well as brain chemistry. Those stress hormones cross the blood-brain barrier. Yet, the question is, do we want to choose Western medicine or Oriental medicine? Allopathic medicine or alternative medicine? Chiropractic is unique because it is based on anatomy, neurology, and biomechanics to improve health by its functions and natural healing ability or so called innate intelligence. I would say all of us need both depending on the conditions and seriousness of the conditions; however, I would choose alternative as a preventative medicine first. It is more cost effective and we should focus on prevention more in the future because we are living in such a toxic world. If you can afford very expensive medical examinations, treatment, or prescriptions, it is up to you. The majority of chronic conditions, including cancer, are preventative. Dr. Oz and other medical doctors also talk about preventative medicine focusing on more nutrition and natural remedies these days. The medical doctors also created an association called functional medicine to see a body as a whole approximately twenty years ago; yet, I think the approach is very much based on chemistry and symptom oriented.

Alternative medicine, on the other hand, includes chiropractic, acupuncture, naturopathic, massage therapy, and so on. The acupuncturists focus on the energy flow in meridian points. Rolfing massage therapists focus on fascia that is a membrane between muscles that some new wave Rolfers practice a form of energy work called "Gamma touch." Cranio-sacral therapy is also focused on energy flow similar to Reiki therapy. Naturopathy is based on more chemical balance as a natural way. Chiropractic care focuses on more structural balance and many mixture chiropractors work on chemical balance with nutritional supplements. It all works! In each therapy, adjustments are all dependent on what structural part we focus on. As I said earlier, the majority of health care approaches have both positive and negative aspects. The question is how much risk a patient will take and how effective the medical intervention will be if we stay the way it is.

Some orthopedic surgeons did research about the cause

of lower back pain and concluded 85 percent of lower back pain is idiopathic (unknown cause). It used to be believed that herniated discs were the major cause of lower back pain; but, 85 percent of lower back surgery fails. What they found is that herniated discs can be taken care of by macrophage, one of the white blood cells, as it recognizes as a foreign object that may disappear by itself. Some individuals may have a major herniated disc without any symptoms. Some may experience excruciating pain with a minimum disc bulge. What I learned through chiropractic seminars about lower back pain is that it is caused by discs, ligament laxity, kidney problems, heart, muscles, particularly psoas muscle tightness that is tightened by the seated position and attaches to all lumbar spine and discs that may pull out the disc(s), meningeal torque, surgical adhesions such as hysterectomy or C-sections, ankle instability, mental stress, brain imbalance, cancer, particularly metastasis to bones, and so on. I have had patients with different causes listed above and will describe some cases in the following section. Sometimes, people experience severe lower back pain without any traumatic incidence. I jump into checking out brain function including TMJ (jaw joint) problems under those circumstances. Even though we focus on the area of complaint, the actual cause is not the area oftentimes. I admit that I cannot fix all the problems, although probably 80 to 90 percent were better. Healing is like peeling onions to remove layers to come up with the cause of the pain. I don't know how many layers you go through every day. One adjustment may not do anything on your accumulated stress to the body, but some patients may think it does not work or the effect does not last and many think the longer the adjustment time, the better. Chiropractic care is not like massage. Muscles have the largest nerve fiber to activate your brain, without knowing the brain functions, massage can be more dangerous to the brain. I still don't know everything about human bodies like everybody else. It is almost impossible to study every field in detail by one person. Our science has not developed to understand everything, yet. The major problem of allopathic approach is not to take care of the cause, just mask the symptoms oftentimes because scientific exams do not reveal so many things on top of focusing on the area of complaints. I do not like to offer a diagnosis to my patients that may threaten a person, particularly if the condition is more serious. I offer them a diagnosis sometimes if it's necessary and when I suspect other serious conditions and refer out to medical doctors to double check with specialists. I don't go by stereotypes by just the areas of pain. I suppose that is one of the causes whereby a patient avoids seeing doctors. Usually a statement by a doctor stays in the patient's mind for a long time. We have a friend who had a major stroke several years ago, I observed his face was so torqued. As he started to recover, his face became closer to his original features. When he choked, I pointed out he may have a problem in his cerebellum. His wife looked at me and told me that he had damaged his throat at the time of the stroke. I would believe it if the doctor had reexamined his throat recently. Everyone has the natural healing power to recover; yet, traditional medicine is still a very reactive care. The majority of patients who stay "Quick and easy" are looking for crisis. "I don't want to cook, I don't want to change my diet, I don't want to do exercise, I don't want to pay high medical expenses, I want to stay a couch potato; I want a free miracle healer!" Is it logical? Is it your American dream? I would say "Good luck!"

Newton's law of universal gravitation simplifies to $F = mg$, where m is the mass of the body and g is a constant vector with an average magnitude of 9.81 m/s². It is similar to that you are walking with a twenty pound bag on the top of your head constantly. Can we see gravity? No! But, it's there. Does it affect the nervous system? Yes! The major factor our brains bear is the gravitational force. As I mentioned in the section, "Plastic, plastic, plasticity," any excitation such as light, sound, touch, eye positions, postures, any joint motions, any activities will activate the brain and change the nervous system to make changes to our body, anatomically and physiologically. I want to buy Nobel Prize winner's findings at an affordable rate. I am a Ross shopper. H. pylori for the cause of stomach ulcer won the Nobel Prize that is more opportunistic infection, some people have it without symptoms during the dormant phase so those patients don't see doctors.

Another problem is that the majority of people think they are fine until pain manifests and still they think the pain will just go away oftentimes. Or people don't really know what kind of doctor to see if it's a minor problem. Some of them are afraid to know, some of them think they cannot afford medical expenses. That is our traditional mind set. People wait for the last minute until they cannot tolerate the pain or symptoms any longer. As they wait, it takes longer or more serious to get better as the body learns to compensate. Pain is the manifestation of accumulated stress to the joints or surrounding structures such as ligaments or muscles on a musculoskeletal system and organ systems. A good example is carpal tunnel syndrome. The median nerve is compressed at the wrist, usually caused by repetitive keyboarding or postural stress like putting your head over the back of your hand. I sometimes do that during seminars when I find I am drooping. Many companies are working on ergonomics to avoid these work related injuries. Of course, there are so many other causes of the pain to differentiate the other disease(s). We repeat the same activities and diet over and over to a specific area to reach the point a person experiences the uncomfortable sensation that is the symptom.

Babies, small kids, elderly patients with fragile bones, and small people most likely cannot take so much pressure or force on their bodies. We cannot apply forceful adjustments to everyone. We modify the procedures for those individuals. Some chiropractors may use force to align the joints that could be harmful, even for big men. What I learned through my personal experiences and some chiropractic classes is that we may not need so much force. The goal is to create the pathways from the area of the problem to activate the brain that sends back the signals to that area of complaint. Does regular chiropractic adjustment create the two-way loop? Yes and no. According to the instructors of the diplomat neurology course, we don't know how neck adjustments by the Diversify technique will affect brain functions. As a matter of fact, many people get injured by neck adjustments and some people are killed by the neck adjustment that is oftentimes done by not well trained people. There are a few people who die from neck manipulation by hair stylists in Taiwan every year. Some physical therapists and even acupuncturists practice some chiropractic adjustments. Some individuals twist their own neck and back to crack their own back like cracking knuckles to alleviate stiffness or pain. That is another habit. Be careful! You are stretching out the ligaments of the joints and affecting your brain functions, resulting in unstable joints by doing it. Why do people out of our profession perform chiropractic? Of course, it works effectively.

Chiropractic philosophy is based on "subluxation" that is also called the pinched nerve or kinked nerve causing "nerve interference" resulting in malfunction of the organs or arms and legs. That is the characteristic of chiropractic. Everyone has a brain and nerves. Pain, aches, stiffness, tingling, numbness, joint position sense, temperature, any sensation is the reaction or activation of nerves. As I said earlier, 90 percent of body functions are controlled by the brain, meaning the central nervous system. Muscles, organs, arms, and legs are all controlled by nerve functions; however, the structural factors are not considered in traditional medicine. Subluxation is not often detected in X-ray or MRI exams even though we can palpate and the patients can feel it. Why does a spine misalign? Functional neurologists (chiropractic neurologists) say that subluxation is a manifestation of the brain function because the cortex controls muscle tone that pulls the spinal segment wherever the area is stressed resulting in the misalignment. People usually don't feel misalignment unless it becomes severe. Some people experience mid-back pain when their stomach pain becomes really bad. Think about the postural stress. How many hours are you seated or cross your legs or put your foot on your thigh every day? Think about how often you use your non-dominant hand to eat or brush your teeth? Those daily activities accumulate and cause the changes to the brain activities that would lead to wearing and tearing, not only of joints, but also brain functions to cause misalignment on your back and internal organ functions. Do you see a dental hygienist when you have toothache? No! We see a dentist for a cavity or toothache. Chiropractors work like dental hygienists and dentists to work on prevention along with treatment.

Many patients who are under chiropractic care for maintenance care do not see medical doctors for medical treatment or go through surgeries as often and many patients could get off some of their medications. I believe these people are responsible for their own health. When we are in pain, we cannot concentrate on what we do and pain may interfere with sleep as well. So many professional athletes and Olympic players have chiropractors as a trainer to reach their peak performance. Why not have chiropractors for regular workers? Working on prevention should be more cost effective in the long term and prevent various diseases by activating the nervous system.

One of my fellow chiropractors told us in a class, he found out there are many more sexual abuse cases of women than he thought. When he does a cranial work, it releases the tension and the patients start crying. When he worked on my cranium, I could not stop crying more than thirty minutes. Those fine articulations of the cranium do not show up on an X-ray or MRI. When we have emotional stress or mental stress, we hold our breath as a natural reaction and tighten up muscles that would shift the cranial or other joint articulations because joints are moved by breathing. Although it is not visible, you may feel the muscle contraction when you are angry or under stress. It is a subtle motion and we cannot perceive the motion unless we apply specific ways to test or carefully palpate. The easiest motion of the bone you can feel is the rib cage as it is designed to expand by inhalation and move back by exhalation as the lungs expand by inhalation. I read a medical article about post traumatic syndrome; patients suffer from various physical problems, but all sorts of doctors have trouble finding the problems. We have not created the diagnostic ways to find out all kinds of disease processes or various conditions, yet. Can we separate any of those factors, including cranial motions, emotional component, digestive stress, or mental stress? No! We have all the factors in one body. People under stress go into adrenal dysfunction, then proceed into adrenal fatigue, and then adrenal exhaustion. The stress hormones known as adrenaline and cortisol affect metabolism, causing blood pressure problems, sugar metabolism, hormonal imbalance, suppress immunity, including natural killer cells that are one of the white blood cells to fight against cancer. Adrenal gland is also one of the causations of high blood pressure. People are under so much stress these days and more adrenal exhaustion is common. Attention deficit disorder and ADHD among adults have been increasing. Early signs of adrenal fatigue and exhaustion are palm sweating, lack of concentration, sleep disturbances, dry lips, trouble organizing items, dry hair, forgetfulness, and so on. Not only chemical interactions inside your body and brain, but shallow breathing also affect the ph levels in your system. The majority of us are acidic even though our systems need to be maintained in a slight alkaline environment inside the body. Cancer cells cannot survive in an alkaline environment. Medical doctors and nutrition specialists talk about chemical imbalance and risk factors on foods, drinks, radiations, and so on. Nonsmokers get lung cancer and smokers do not always get lung cancer. How can we narrow down on chemistry only? Everything around you can be a risk factor to develop cancer and we are living in such a toxic environment. When we palpate your body, we feel, and you feel the tightness, or pain before any blood test manifest. The point I want to make is working on prevention is more effective and sufficient than waiting for crisis.

Many people still think chiropractors are back doctors. One Saturday afternoon, a big American guy walked into my office and asked me, "Can you adjust my back?" and I replied to him "Yes!" He looked at me (I am about 5 feet and 100 pounds) and said, "My chiropractor is a big guy. I don't think you can crack my back . . . " and he walked away. The SOT and STO use wedge-shape blocks to adjust the pelvis so that I don't have so much trouble adjusting my patients. My youngest patient was a two-day-old new born baby who had colic. The application of less than a half pound of pressure that would be much less than when you lift up a baby corrected the baby's back. The baby created noise and smiled back while I was holding the baby less than five minutes. My oldest patient was about ninety-one years old with severe osteoporosis and with hearing impairment along with balancing problems. Cranial nerve eight in the middle ear is responsible for hearing and balance. Where is the connection to it? The neck and kidneys! It took me a couple visits to see improvement and I continued the care for several visits. Significant improvement was achieved, but it does not mean I "cured" and I know it will come back because nephron in the kidneys and joints degenerates by aging. Can we stop the degeneration process of aging? No, I don't think so, but we can delay the process by how we maintain our bodies. The majority of patients look for an instant cure even if they wait for a long time to get the pain. I don't know how many layers of onion you have to come up with the symptoms, please give me a break to get rid of your symptoms in one or two adjustments. Think about the meaning of the word, patient and patience. I suppose patients need to learn patience. Sometimes, patients have multiple diagnostic conditions before they come into my office, not necessarily physical conditions, some are more emotionally linked conditions such as panic attack disorder or post traumatic syndrome. Those emotionally linked conditions are really tough to deal with even for medical doctors because we don't have diagnostic machines to detect all sorts of your problems. I suppose asthma is also closely linked with emotional issues. I had a case study that my patient complained of an asthmatic type of symptoms and was on inhaler; I adjusted her to improve her respiration for several visits or more, but still could not get results. I thought about it, why? then, I asked my patient "What kind of activity triggers your symptoms?" She replied she was sitting in smoke at a casino for hours that initiated bad coughing. The next time was right after she opened the oven and smoke came out! "Aha!" I adjusted her allergy by TBM that cleared up her symptoms. Any kind of allergy is associated with sugar metabolism that screws up your system to induce bacterial reactions in your system. Watch your sweet tooth and be careful for your own self-diagnosis that may result in misguiding your doctor! This is my viewpoint as a doctor.

My tallest patient was about 6 feet 7 inches tall and around

250 lbs. with shoulder pain. When I checked his shoulder joints, he could not resist and got upset, telling me, "How can you pull my arm down?" I know how it articulates, so I adjusted the shoulder joints. It may hold for a while, it may not come back for years. I do check vital signs, I do orthopedic exams, I do neurological exams, and I observe and palpate. It all depends on how the patient uses their body. The heaviest patient was over 300 lbs. and I used blocks to protect my shoulder and my back. I like to get agreement with my patients. Usually, my patients say, "It's right there!" Some procedures can be painful . . . Good pain does not last so long, but bad pain lasts longer. Kids cry when it hurts. Which do you prefer? Oftentimes, a massage hurts when we build up lactic acid that is the end product of metabolism. There is a new invention to take out the lactic acid from the muscles by nitrogen gas at much lower than freezing points. Some Olympic athletes and professional athletes started to use it under chiropractic care. For regular people, massage therapists, chiropractors, or physical therapists work to reduce the tension and lactic acid. Same thing, but chiropractors work on nerves on top of muscles and joints. What structure would make you move? Joints along with muscles! What structure controls muscles including organ muscles to move joints? Nerves! We all have nerves! We all have chemistry in the system, but, we have different chemistries because no one eats the same thing. We all have minds and emotions that are different for each individual as each person reacts differently and everyone has different stress. The SOT research division created the protocol for fibromyalgia by cranial manipulations without any supplementation, usually ten office visits to reduce pain. Recent findings indicate estrogen is closely linked with pain, but chemical balance is not only the cause of pain. One of my fibromyalgia patients had a blood test after my cranial work and the test indicated all inflammatory

factors were dropped down to normal levels and the majority of pain was gone. The SOT research division created protocols for pregnancy that I would include infertility, miscarriage, and the reposition of breech babies. If you have problems on fertility, ask yourself if you cross your legs, sit in front of the TV or computer, have stress levels, mood swings, PMS? Female reproductive organs are not quite stable because it is just supported by thin membranes to keep its position in the abdominal cavity. By crossing the legs, the thin membrane can be pulled to one side and may result in malposition of the ovaries and womb. Those problems are treatable under chiropractic care in conjunction with nutrition and some modifications on your diet. I have had patients get pregnant following chiropractic adjustment, and I have repositioned breech babies, I have induced contraction when an OB/GYN doctor could not. I would say teamwork makes our life much easier. The SOT doctors created pediatric classes for autism, dyslexia, learning disorders, and so on. We look for which nerve is affecting and causing pain or symptoms. From the viewpoint as preventative care, traditional medicine seems to be reactive care because medical doctors are looking for a pathology such as tumors and diseases. I would say future medicine should focus on more preventative care because what we want is to secure our health along with function in our lifespans. Staying on a poor diet without preventative care, regular exercise and regular checkups, we are looking for higher risks to develop diseases in this toxic world. We all need to have both scientific measures and functional measures to prevent and function to secure our health. "Quick and easy" medications or surgeries may help to mask the pain and functions at the time; however, there are many medically induced conditions as well. A doctor who had knee surgery got an infection and ended up with an amputation. Western medicine seems to have higher risk factors and is invasive if you wait for the last minute. Think about the lawsuits against these medications and surgeries. I suppose that is the major reason for the increase in the cost of medical fees and medications. If you stay "quick and easy," you have higher risks in the long term and it costs you a lot more and you may end up travelling around to see specialists, particularly in the United States. One of my friends who is a senior citizen went to an urgent care center when she had radiating pain down her left arm and the side of her trunk. She was concerned it could be her heart problem. The cardiologist did blood tests, just general screening tests, not specific to the heart and had X-rays taken. She stayed at the hospital for six hours and they concluded that she had a pinched nerve in her neck. She showed me the explanation of benefit (EOB) from her insurance company. My mouth dropped because the hospital charge was over $6,700 and the insurance company paid $370 on top of her deductible for $50. How can a hospital or doctors pay all the expenses? Another friend who had an infection went to a hospital as he had a high fever that did not drop down for a couple of weeks. As he was unemployed, he did not have a health insurance at that time, and his doctor did a CT scan and blood tests and other expensive exams. Everything was negative. He could not get adequate care and ended up paying unnecessary medical examination fees as outrageous medical charges. The majority of people in the United States depend on cars to commute, for grocery shopping, and for traveling, one car accident could be very critical to the nervous system. I had a patient who was involved in a car accident with a drunk driver. He lost consciousness and one side of his entire body was black and blue so that he was carried into the hospital. He had a CT scan and the doctor told him that he was fine. CT scans and MRI exams are used to look for pathology like tumors or hemorrhages, and do not show nerve damage nor fine articulation of joint structure. He developed lower back pain later as a result. Many patients who are involved in car accidents develop so many health problems later and they are not treated well because we don't have great diagnostic machines to detect all sorts of nerve reactions. Since the neck is very close to your brain, it makes sense to develop various symptoms depending on your eye and neck positions at the time of impact. Acupuncture works for pain controlled by meridian points, but do they work for nerve impingement? Not specifically! Massage therapists work on muscle aches that feel good. Does it work for joint pain? No! Neurological signs also affect muscles. Medications may work to mask the pain or symptoms temporally, but may not work and you need to think about the side effects of these medications. The question is, how much can a patient take risks on in their health care plan? Which chiropractic technique has less risk and is more effective? Concerning the anatomical structures, we have brain and spinal cord, meningeal system, blood circulations, lymphatic system, CSF, organs on top of nervous system. The brain controls 90 percent, that's the majority. Where is the other 10 percent? I think the sacrum as an autonomic nervous system. Which techniques cover all components? SOT and STO. I am not saying that other chiropractic techniques do not work. All chiropractic techniques work, but applications are much wider if we consider these anatomical structures. If magnets would work for you and for your patients, that's fine and best for you. Please keep up your good work on your patients. If AK technique works for you, that's fine. As long as you and your patients are happy about it, it is not my business. Now, the question is, if a patient has meningeal torque, stress over the lumbar and sacrum would result in further torque by side posture adjustments? I would say yes, it would. I have bumped into a couple of patients with bad lower back pain who were adjusted by one of the top functional neurologists and both of them got worse from side posture adjustments. I hear both the positive side and the negative side about chiropractic. I had a patient who was adjusted by HIO and SAM (spinal analysis machine) and both of them got injured by forceful adjustment repeatedly. The SOT has modified ways to adjust cervical regions as stair steps by compressing neck joints and drawing a figure eight that synchronizes to the brain activity. The STO has the dynamic stretch to flick the neck joints. We adjust knees by blocking without any forceful adjustments. How many chiropractors have injured their shoulders from side posture adjustments? If you do side posture adjustment, particularly over the sacrum, you have higher risks to cause injury to the patients as well as your own shoulder and you limit yourself to adjusting a wide range of population groups. The question is, why do chiropractic schools not teach less risky, more effective techniques first? Why do we stick with Newton physics while our science has already shifted to Quantum physics? I believe Dr. M. L. Rees is right because everything in our body at the cellular level is vibrating. The majority of therapies have been shifting toward energy work. The following section describes some of the case studies on how bodies were affected by emotional stress, how one joint affected other joint structures, how organs affected spinal joints and mechanisms and how the body compensated. Many patients focus on pain and drop the maintenance care and develop different subsequent problems, not only American people, but also other ethnic groups. However, American people are more oriented toward a "quick and easy" fix, and do not prioritize their budget on their health. Diagnostic tests do not show all of your complaints, particularly fine cranial motions, sacrum articulations, and the small muscles to rotate your spine.

Most good dentists will tell you keeping your original teeth as long as you can is the best. Good orthopedic surgeons tell you to keep your original joints as long as you can. How do you keep your car running at its best? Regular maintenance and tune-ups, isn't it? Chiropractic care is like a tune-up to activate your brain as well as your organs. My answer for the choice of chiropractic technique is components of both SOT and STO; they are not easy techniques to master and take years and years of training. My final answer is SOT/STO! Din, din, din, din din!

Some websites to check are www.SOTOUSA.com and www.SORSI.com.

Although I want to support STO doctors, I cannot list the website because some doctors lost their licenses in some states by discrimination and bias to the technique. I am aware that more and more people are looking for this type of gentle energy work and healers; however, I need to protect their licenses. If you want this technique approved in your state, you may want to contact the chiropractic board examiner in your state.

If you cannot locate SOT doctors nearby and have problems, especially neurological problems, you may want to check out the website.

They are specialized in neurological problems such as ADD/ADHD, Parkingson's, stroke and so forth, Please see www.carrickinstitute.org and ACNB.com (American Chiropractic Neurology Board).

Many of ADD/ADHD patients, autistic kids, dyslexia, and other neurological conditions are reversed by brain balancing techniques and they created vestibular courses for those who suffer from dizziness, balancing problems, and so forth.

*Disconnected Kids* by Dr. Robert Melillo is also an interesting book to read. This book is about children with neurological disorders including autism.

One out of eight kids in the United States has those neurological problems. Kids are our future and we are in such a health crisis, now.

Those are the associations I belong to and support, but I don't want to discriminate against other chiropractic techniques. Please check out the yellow pages, Yelp, the Better Business Bureau or any other websites to locate your chiropractor.

# MY REPORT OF FINDINGS

It started when a weird bird came to my car. I had a lunch with my friend and talked about the color of the car. I was driving a burgundy SUV at that time, which was a favorite target of birds and there were bird droppings all over the car. I thought the color of the car might not be good and I should buy a lighter color next time. When I walked out of the restaurant and went back to my car, I noticed a bird was standing on the wiper blade facing toward me and looking at me. I expected that the bird would fly away when I started the engine. It did not go away so that I started to drive and left the parking lot. The bird was still there, looking at me and I started to drive on the street to go back home. Then the bird turned around, tilted its tail up, and contracted its end. "Oh, my God! It will poop over the windshield!" The bird was standing on the wiper against the wind that was blowing its feathers for several minutes from the restaurant to my home. I ignored the bird and went into my house and came out to go back to my office after one hour or so. The bird was still there. I thought, *maybe this bird has injured its wing and can not fly* . . . So I tried to touch its foot and the bird stepped sideways on the wiper. I found the poop on my windshield. Shoot! I tried to hold its leg, but the bird jumped off and up to the roof on the second floor and was still looking at me. "Hmm . . . It could fly. It was so weird, but I needed to go back to my office. Around that time, my father was sick and was at the terminal stage of cancer. I called my sister who lived nearby my parents' house and told the story of the weird bird. "I thought the bird could be the spirit of my father saying good-bye to me." She replied, "It's so weird. It must be him because he is so weird." I also told her, "Give him the supplements that I brought in last time quickly. You are so slow, moving like a slug. I am a snail; I can hide in the shell, so that I can roll down and move very quickly!" He survived another four months, but I got case study patients of dystonia one after another after the weird bird came. I interpreted the bird as a messenger and I think it's me!

A seventeen-year-old girl came to my clinic with a strange gait problem. According to her mother, she walked on her tip toes. She hesitated to show me her abnormal gait for a while and I asked her mother to put on her flip flops. She started to trust in me and showed me the way she walked without modifying the gait. I showed her the YouTube video, "Lion sleeps tonight!" the cartoon video with the hippo singing the song and the dog dancing in front of the hippo. It is very funny, but the coordination of the dog dancing is very good. I told her and her mother, "In your case, you have a problem with coordination." When I checked out her gaze, her head was tilted down to the left and forward. "Oh, my God! I have never seen a patient like that . . . " and I checked out her vascular system. Her left hand was significantly paler than her right hand.

I called one of my neuro-mates (one of my classmates for neurology class) and told him about my findings. He responded that I might need to refer her to a vascular specialist. I did not know about the head tilt around that time as I had not taken vestibular classes. I blocked her as Category I and did cranial work later, but the patient's mother said, "I don't think a chiropractor can correct the problem, I will take her to a podiatrist for surgery!" I don't know what happened to the girl. The other findings on neurological tests clearly indicated that her problem was associated with brain function. Patients just don't know how the body connects to each other.

On Monday of the following week, another patient came in with a chief complaint of severe lower back pain. He told me that he was in a wheelchair for a week before he came into my office and he could only walk with a cane and with assistance from his wife. He could not lie down on the adjustment table due to his severe lower back pain and severe muscle contractions along with the inability to straighten his left hip joint. He was screaming swear words and moaning. It was very hard to do some physical exams . . . what I could think of was doing the knee tendon reflex in a seated position for the exam. I tapped the patient's knee tendon and he almost jumped off the adjustment table and his left lower leg jumped up. "Oh my God!" I was feeling my adrenal hormone boosting up. That is the neurological sign of an upper motor neuron lesion meaning that there was a brain problem. What I could think of at that time for the treatment was to touch his tammy to boost the energy. I checked his knee reflex again after five minutes of treatment. He did not jump and his reflex was normal. On the following day, he came back and the patient reported, "I don't know what you did, but I feel much better!" His wife said with a smile, "Yes! He is much better, like a very active elderly person." The patient was still on the cane, walking around with an abrupt gait, but much quicker than before. I checked his knee tendon reflex, again. It was still normal, but the patient could not lie down on the adjustment table due to severe muscle contractions in his left lower body. I did the same procedure, again and noticed he had a tender spot on the left side of his skull. I put my finger in his mouth and stretched the membrane from his mouth. I also advised the patient to take CoQ10, 300 mg a day. I scheduled the patient two days later, but he cancelled the appointment. Two weeks later, he came back without the cane and was walking normally. He could lie down on the adjustment table without any trouble so I blocked him as

Category I. He reported that he had taken CoQ10, 600 mg a day. There's nothing wrong with it. The higher dosage of CoQ10, the better result you may get for neurological conditions if you can afford it. He also told me that he was swimming obsessively. The skin is the largest organ, so swimming in a high content of chlorinated water may have induced a neurological condition like this . . . I talked to myself, *what did I do to this patient?*

I took another neurology class in the meantime. The instructor lectured on how to conduct an initial consultation. Using OPQRST . . . O stands for onset of symptom, P stands for provoking or palliative factors and blah, blah, blah. He also added another pneumonic, MDSHIT. The M stands for medications the patient is taking, for what conditions, D stands for diagnostic conditions and so forth. These pneumonic help me a lot.

On the following Monday, another patient came in with a chief complaint of her right foot cramping with pain along with the inability to spread her right toes, she had gait disturbance where her right leg swirled and she had left hand tremor. She had traveled to numerous neurologists, but the neurologists could not find anything, so she had ended up at the Parkinson's Institute. The pneumonic really helped me, so I did minimum physical exams to confirm the diagnosis. Bingo! I blocked her as Category I that is a category system to classify the block positions; this category is associated with the meningeal system. I adjusted her spine and adjusted her cranium to spread her sagittal suture on the first visit. Voila! All her symptoms were gone. I talked to myself, again, *what did I do to this patient?*

I thought about these case studies . . . and played the computer game called Free Cell, similar to solitaire game. I hooked up with this game for years and played for hours.

I questioned myself, "Why do I play this game over and over?" I came up with an answer.

"Ah! This game is the neurology for me. Our brain and

human body have certain pathways to connect. What we need is to align the numbers in order and match the suits like this game!" Thomas Edison stated that a genius is 1 percent of inspiration and 99 percent of perspiration. In my case, it was 1 percent of inspiration and 99 percent of playing the game. If a person can explain something very well, people will call that person a genius. If a person cannot explain to others well, people call the person crazy. Probably, I am still on the side of a crazy person.

I will briefly explain my theory for regular people. The sacral bone is situated in the center of your butt, the pelvic bones on both sides connect to the sacral bone by ligaments, and the joints are called the SI joints. The entire spine sits on the top of the sacral bone. When you cross your legs, the side of the SI (sacro iliac) joint you lift up your leg needs to move backward. This is biomechanics. The nervous system, particularly the central nervous system is important because it is your brain and spinal cord that connects the entire body, so the spinal cord is protected by three layers of membrane called the meningeal system that wraps around the entire brain and spinal cord. The most outer layer is called the dura mater, dura means tough in Latin so that it does not stretch out like a vinyl sheath; the middle layer is called the arachnoid mater; and the most internal membrane is called the pia mater that is almost fused into the spinal cord and brain. Cerebrospinal fluid, or CSF, circulates between the pia mater and the arachnoid mater against gravitational force. How does the body circulate the fluid? It must have a pumping mechanism. The sacrum and occipital bones at the bottom and back of your skull, act like a pump by breathing. When you cross your legs, the erector muscles, nerves coming out from the sacral area, and joint mechanoreceptors transfer all input to the occipital bone. What happens when you cross your legs? It brings your pelvic bone backward. Yes, it creates an asymmetrical SI joint motion that creates a wobbling motion from the sacrum, which results in the occipital bone that receives the motion from the sacrum with a synchronized motion. Yes, it wobbles and tilts! The wobbling motion from the sacrum creates the wobbling motion in the occiput and the parietal bone sitting on the top of occipital bone also wobbles, which results in jamming the joint on the top of the head. The asymmetrical wobbling motion results in stress to the membrane system inside the skull that results in the membrane system torqueing along with changes on dynamics of fluid motion of the CSF that may lead to the compression of brain parts. This is the philosophy of SOT. It makes sense to me. Does it make sense to you?

In SOT, Dr. De Jarnette did not explain well enough and taught that the indicators, such as lower back pain, are associated with the joint or so called sagittal suture on the top of the head. The question, why, drove me crazy and I drove my teachers crazy! The top of the head in the midline coincides with a neurological mapping of the so called homunculus, indicating the lower back and legs. Cool!

Here is my theory in my third language, also called medical jargon. Chiropractors and some neurologists may be interested in my theory. The case study three is switched over and case one is another case added for this book.

## ABSTRACT:

The spinal manipulative treatment for dystonia, which is a neurological condition and classified as a movement disorder characterized by aberrant motion, was studied.

Oftentimes, dystonia affects extremities causing unilateral muscle contraction.

Sacro-occipital technique or SOT was founded by Dr. De Jarnette, Soft Tissue Orthopedic or STO was founded by Dr. M.L. Rees and chiropractic functional neurology by Dr. Frederic

Carrick were the applications for the adjustment.

Some dystonic cases were studied to determine its causation and assessment.

## INTRODUCTION:

Genetic factors, history of trauma, mental disorders, and metabolic disorders are considered as the causation of dystonia; however, the etiology and the pathology on this condition are not understood well. The following case studies and anatomical corrections have led to other possible causations of this movement disorder.

## CASE STUDIES:

Case One: A forty-three-year-old Asian female visited our clinic with a chief complaint of right foot cramps, gait disturbances, and a left hand resting tremor. She complained the toes on her right foot were cramped, causing pain and the inability to spread her toes.

She had a history of a fall on an icy road, landing on her buttock approximately twenty-five years earlier. The patient had visited numerous neurologists, but no significant abnormalities were detected so that she was referred to a Parkinson's institute for semi-annual check-ups. She reported that she had surgery to remove 96 percent of her thyroid gland approximately twenty years prior when she was diagnosed as having Grave's disease.

Placement of a small sheet of paper over bilateral fingers that exaggerate the motion confirmed her left hand resting tremor. Observation of her gait revealed a circumductive gait in which she swirled her entire right leg. Kemp's test revealed slight muscle contractions on the right. Palpation over the pelvic region revealed muscle spasms in her left buttock region and tenderness over her right SI joint and right Achilles tendon.

These findings are also part of the SOT (sacro-occipital technique) indicators for block positions so called category system. Tenderness or spasticity in a buttock area is called a "dollar sign" as it resembles the size of silver dollar coin due to the piriformis muscle contractions. Achilles tendon tenderness is called heel tension and one of the indicators for Category I. Both muscles are the posterior muscles below T6 that indicate the lack of inhibition from the contralateral cortex so that the patient was blocked as Category I. Sacro-occipital technique cranial palpation revealed tenderness in her sagittal suture that was jammed in and was spread at the same time. The patient's right toes were spread and the tremor was stopped immediately after the first adjustment. Over 300 mg of CoQ10 per day was recommended after the first visit.

This case involved both metabolic and emotional components and took several visits; her swirl gait came back along with her regular period. I referred her to an endocrinologist.

Case Two: A thirty-two-year-old white male with a chief complaint of severe low back pain visited our clinic. He had no history of any traumatic incidents and no episodes of lower back pain. His left side of musculature in his left lower body was severely contracted so that the patient was not able to straighten his lower back and his left hip joint. He was in a wheelchair for a week prior to this visit. He came in with a cane and assisted by his wife. The patient was not able to lie down in a prone position due to severe pain and the muscle contraction. Deep Tendon Reflex also known as Muscle Spindle Reflex is a part of neurological exams to examine reflex to differnciate Upper Motor Neuron Lesion that means more brain problems or Lower Motor Neuron lesions that means more peripheral nerve problems. We tap the tendons at elbow, forearm, just below your knee cap and Achilles tendons with a reflex hammer. When we find positive finding on the test, we perform different tests to specify which part of brain, which spinal segment, which nerve is affected to cause the problem on the patient. In this case, MSR on the left patellar revealed hyperreflexia and the patient reported he experienced electric sensations all way up to his head when his left patellar was tapped.

In this case scenario, mechanical correction by SOT blocks was impossible due to the severity of the muscle contraction and the severe pain. Therefore, adjustment was a form of energy work founded by Dr. M. L. Rees on the initial visit and the following visit, which normalized the DTR on the left patellar after the first visit. He came back with a cane on the following day and his left lower body was still severely contracted.

Palpation over his cranium revealed the tenderness over the left superior nuchal line, approximately halfway between the mastoid process and the foramen magnum that is the indicator for tentorium torque. Using the sacro-occipital technique of intraoral manipulation (contacting behind the last molar with a coated finger and gently pulling along the gum line from posterior to anterior; please refer to the discussion for further explanations) to correct the tentorium torque was rendered on the second visit. Over 300 mg of CoQ10 per day was recommended. He accidentally took 600 mg per day. He came back without the cane and no discomfort after two weeks.

Case Three: A forty-six-year-old white male with a chief complaint of right lower leg pain along with difficulty in moving his right foot visited our clinic. No history of trauma. He has experienced this sharp pain in his right lower leg and foot three to four times since last year. His blood pressure was 132/70 on the right and 132/82 on the left in a seated position, 132/82 on the right and 132/82 on the left in a standing position. The straight leg raise (SLR) test was positive indicating a right posterior muscle contraction of 60/90 and 85/90 on the left. He was blocked as Category I in the prone position and sagittal suture was spread on the first visit. His SLR test was still positive on the second visit (a week later). Motor testing on his right biceps brachii was weak. After the SOT cat one blocking, a fast stretch on his right fingers and wrist to correct hemisphericity was rendered on the second visit that resolved the SLR finding.

Case Four: A forty-three-year-old Asian female with a history of trauma over her bilateral SI joints from a side posture chiropractic adjustment approximately seven years ago prior to this visit. She reported that she completely lost control of her urination and bowel movements after the side posture adjustment over her sacrum and developed bilateral spastic paralysis in both her legs. This case has multiple lesions in her brain and cord compression as she complained of problems completing urination. She falls to various directions by the Romberg test. Her fingers to nose, arm position sense is unremarkable. A blind spot test indicates bilateral parietal and temporal abnormalities. Palpation revealed bilateral SI joints edema (worse on the left).

Her sacrum is tilted into the ilium on the left. Her cranium is torqued as her right mastoid process is posterior and her left parietal is anterior in comparison to the contralateral side. Her vibration sense is decreased in her left medial ankle. She has decreased dorsiflexion of bilateral ankle (worse on the left.) The application of a tuning fork to stimulate the vestibular pass way exacerbated her symptoms such as tachycardia and incontinence. Placing the tuning fork to her right ear in the standing position resulted in sacral movement through the homologous column; however, it does not have a specific vector to correct SI joint articulation. Inhibition to the parasympathetic innervations by sacral misalignment resulted in increasing FOF (frequency of firing) to the left IML to the right cortex that resulted in the tachycardia and incontinence.

Results: Not resolved, yet. It's me! I wanted to know what happened after the adjustment. I was better before the car accident this year and happy because I learned a lot.

DISCUSSION:

The SOT classification for Category I is accompanied with meningeal torque. The meningeal system is such a broad membrane system that encapsulates the whole brain and the entire spinal cord and then anchors at the base of coccyx by filum terminale. In order to circulate cerebrospinal fluid (CSF) against gravitational force, a body needs to have a pumping mechanism. The sacrum and occiput have a reciprocal motion by respiration for pumping. This is a SOT philosophy. Joint motion on sacroiliac should be symmetrical; however, it does not always produce symmetrical motion due to joint misalignment. The asymmetrical joint motion creates a wobbling motion from the unilateral SI joint that transmits to the occiput through joint mechanoreceptors, erector spinae muscle groups, and so on. A pair of parietal bones that situate over the occipital bone through the lambdoid suture merges at the sagittal suture that could be jammed in or separated due to altered SI joint motions. Most often it is jammed in, based on my clinical observations. Since a dural membrane is such a tough membrane that does not stretch out, it may affect the various areas of brain if it's torqued. The hydrostatic pressure created by the CSF flow may cause further torque of the dural membrane. Dynamics of fluid motion created by the joint motion of the occiput and sacrum pumping mechanism may result in the compression to the areas of the brain adjacent to the membrane structure. The sacral motions by respirations, daily activities, postural stress, chemical imbalance, and even emotional stress affect the SI joint articulation due to sympathetic and parasympathetic activities so that it may take a long period of time to manifest a symptom.

In the first case scenario, the falx cerebri was torqued. The dural membrane compressing the most adjacent structures such as supplementary, premotor, and primary motor cortex were lined up along with the sagittal suture. The prefrontal motor cortex rostral to supplementary motor cortex has the highest inhibitory motor function that was also accessible from the metopic suture. From the sagittal suture where the membrane attaches, the most midline structure associated with the leg, the torque was corrected. The putamen received from the motor cortex synapsed to the thalamus via the globus paridus interna resulted in inhibition of the motor function in her right leg and left hand tremor.

In the second case scenario, his left tentorium was torqued, affecting the adjacent structures above the left tentorium such as the parahippocampal gyrus and /or the occipitotemporal gyrus or left cerebellum. Concerning the mechanism of the correction, the posterior margin of the tentorium attaches to the interior of the occipital bone in the area of the superior nuchal line. The falx cerebri attaches to the middle superior of the tentorium at the posterior and at the crista galli at the anterior of the skull. It lines the interior of the posterior skull being laterally attached along the petrous portions of the temporal bones. The anterior ends then cross and are attached to the anterior and posterior clinoid processes at the sella turcica of the sphenoid bone. On inhalation, the sphenoid bone flexes anterior and inferior, elevating the clinoid processes on the posterior part of the sphenoid, the squamous portion of the occiput flexes approximating the falx cerebri. The temporal bones flare externally and rotate inferiorly, extending the tentorium laterally. On exhalation, these bone structures and the tentorium reposition back to the neutral position. These motions during respiration draw the tentorium laterally on inhalation and extend its anterior to posterior dimensions on exhalation. When the tentorium is torqued, these marginal areas would bear additional tension since the dural membrane does not stretch. Because of the approximation of the falx cerebri and the lateral draw of the tentorium, the most motion created by the respiration is the medial rim of the tentorium due to instability because there is no attachment to any bone structures. From the medial rim, the opposing vector force to maintain the balance is the other end of the membrane where it attaches to the occipital bone. Therefore, an accessible area to detect the tentorium torque has been found at the superior nuchal line of the occipital bone where the tentorium and falx cerebri join. An indicator for the tentorium torque is tenderness approximately halfway between the mastoid process and the foramen magnum on the superior nuchal line on either or both sides. For correction of tentorium torque, the lateral pterygoid process is moved in response to associated respiratory application as needed. If corrected on inhalation, it is taken laterally and posteriorly. If corrected on exhalation, it is taken on the lateral pterygoid process behind the last molar medially and anteriorly. Moving the pterygoid process incorrectly affects the tentorium attachments to the clinoid processes of the sella turcica of the sphenoid acting to further stress the tentorium. (It is much easier to watch the computerized simulation model for cranial and meningeal motion to understand the concept if you are interested in this.)

In the third case scenario, this patient had a falx cerebri torque accompanied with hemisphericity. This case, however, indicated that structural correction through meningeal torque adjustment was needed before the hemisphericity correction. The reduction of pelvic torsion and its aiding in improving hamstring muscle tone as well as gait had good biological plausibility. Treatment anticipated to affect cortical hemisphericity (fast stretch on his right fingers and wrist) was rendered based on the increased standing diastolic blood pressure on the right, the increased right hamstring muscle tone, and the reduced right biceps brachii as well as the right gluteus medius strength.

In the fourth case, this involves cranial volt torque along with a sacrum tilt. Because of the cranial torque, the whole intracranial meningeal system must be twisted, compressing multiple areas of the brain such as the right frontal lobe, the vestibular systems bilaterally due to the paramedian nucleus and the right pyramidal area. Considering the tuning fork application to activate the right vestibular system, it probably induced sacral movement through the homologous column; however, it does not have a specific vector to correct SI joint articulation. Inhibition to the parasympathetic innervations by sacral misalignment resulted in increase of FOF (frequency of firing) to the left IML to the right frontal cortex that resulted in tachycardia and incontinence. In regards to her initial bowel and urinary incontinence, the side posture adjustment resulted in compression of or damage to either or both the pelvic and the sacral splanchnic nerve that exits from S2, S3, S4 and regulates the rectum and the urinary bladder. Over a period of time, these reciprocal sacrum and occipital movements created further torque that would explain why dystonia progressed as time went by.

CONCLUSION:

According to the research by the Carrick Institute for Graduate Study for Neurology, dystonia is due to mesencephalic and/or basal ganglionic lesions and may be accompanied with hemisphericity. It is a general idea; however, the actual lesion may vary depending on a case. These outcomes suggest that dystonia could be induced by the meningeal torque. The actual lesion could be the area compressed by the meningeal torque, not necessarily a simple area, it could be multiple lesions; yet, the meningeal system does not appear on an MRI. To confirm my theory, a myelogram with contrast media may show the meningeal torque along with CSF. This method, however, is way risky to a patient and medical doctors are inhibited to perform the procedure. Further investigation is necessary for these case studies.

Comments: I did not include the neurotransmitter reactions and enzymatic reactions at the synaptic junctions on this theory as the chemical portion inside of the brain. I focused more on the anatomical and neurological explanations in this theory.

**Planter fasciitis and CSF:** A forty-one-year-old white female with a chief complaint of left heel pain without any history of running on uneven surfaces that might cause a tension on her planter fascia.

She has a history of ulcerative colitis and I co-managed her ulcerative colitis along with a prescription.

Intervention: H-line and Aim line created by M.L. Rees corresponding to the area to flow and to balance the CSF and the adjustment of her tarsal bones.

Discussion: Some research indicated a stained CSF was placed back to the lumbar region and found the cell at the left wrist after one hour. CSF travels all over the body so that the fluid balance may be the key to correcting the patient's problematic area. She experienced excruciating pain so she saw her medical doctor and was told that she had planter fasciitis.

I further noticed the foot pain could be associated with colon function associated with the nerve coming out from the sacrum two through four to innervate the colon that coincides with the dermatome down to the Achilles tendon to pull the planter fascia. Usually, the patient's history tells us where to go.

Result: The patient reported that she did not experience the excruciating heel pain.

Conclusion: Planter fasciitis is a common condition, but the area of the problem may not be the major cause like in this case. The history and palpation over the planter fascia are crucial for adjustment.

**Knee Pain:** A sixty-nine-year-old white female with a chief complaint of moderate lower back and knee pain. She had a history of a total hysterectomy and knee surgery after a bad fall. She had difficulty in walking that required her to use a cane, as well as difficulty in getting up from a chair and staying asleep due to her knee pain.

Intervention: She had Category III blocking on the first visit and knee adjustment. The patient could get up from the chair without any problem after the first visit. Her knee pain still remained after a few visits so that her ovaries were adjusted which reduced the knee pain significantly.

Discussion: The history of a total hysterectomy made me think, "Why?" This is similar to the phantom pain that a patient experiences in an amputated body part. Even if an organ or a body part is surgically removed, the nerve connection is still there and the brain perceives the nerve connection from the body part. That is the mechanism of phantom pain. The nerve connection to the knee and ovaries are coming from the same nerve root as L3. I further noticed knee pain was also related to colon function as of S2 behind the knee that coincides with the dermatome and the nerve distribution that goes behind the knee.

Result: The patient came back after two months without her cane and reported that her knee pain had woken her up only once since then.

Comment: I also worked on her surgical scar tissues to break adhesions with advanced STO. I have seen a patient who had an injury in his hand and had surgery. He developed major adhesions in his hand that resulted in his left hand being in the fist position and surgeons could not operate on him after that because the surgical repair would result in more adhesions.

The patient had had the fist position for twenty years and his hand was almost completely open when I saw him at my teacher's office. Pretty cool! Teamwork makes our life much easier.

**Ankle pain:** A forty-eight-year-old Asian female with a chief complaint of left ankle pain without any traumatic incidence.

Intervention: Ankle and teeth adjustment.

Result: The patient reported that she no longer has pain in her ankle.

I had a patient with a headache; I adjusted her ankle and her headache was gone.

The foot bone connects to the shin bone, the shin bone connects to the knee bone is very true. All body parts are connected, all the way up to the head.

**Hip joint pain:** A fifty-three-year-old Asian female with an excruciating right hip joint pain.

Intervention: I adjusted the hip joint first in different ways in the first few visits that helped the hip joint pain a little, but the pain came back. I checked her pubic bone because there was a misaligned SI joint.

Discussion: Hip joint and shoulder joints are relatively hard to correct by chiropractors because those joints are attached to so many other muscles from different regions and other joints. I further investigated other manuals on different cases of hip joint pain. I found out the hip joints are associated with colon functions that explains why people in their mid-fifties experience hip joint pain.

Result: The patient is happy!

**Shoulder pain:** A fifty-five-year-old Asian female with a chief complaint of shoulder pain on both sides, along with a popping, cricking sound when in motion.

Objective Findings: All shoulder joints are unstable on both sides.

Intervention: Category II along with Category II cranial basic.

Discussion: This patient exhibited bilateral all shoulder joints misalignment. Bilateral means quadra equina, spinal cord . . . okay cervical cord above . . . Cupping bilateral occipital bone to activate the bilateral cerebellum and bilateral frontal bone . . . Voila! All shoulder joints are aligned. This patient came back with unilateral (one side) shoulder popping sound exhibiting an anterior glenohumeral joint on that side. I did an intraoral cranial work application at that time on the same side. I also got another patient who complained of right shoulder pain and both shoulder joints were unstable and did this procedure.

Result: These patients reported that they did not experience shoulder pain or any popping sound.

**Diarrhea and Constipation:** Case One: A thirty-eight-year-old Asian female came to my office with a complaint of mid-back pain and frequent diarrhea in the past half-year. She also complained of high cholesterol even though she had been modifying her diet along with an exercise program in the past several years in order to prevent prescription drugs. She was also concerned that she might have hyperthyroidism because her mother had bulging eyes without any abnormality on the blood tests.

Objective findings: Blood tests for the thyroid panel indicated fluctuation patterns in the last few years. When her stress level was significantly high, free T3 and T4 were slightly elevated and dropped down into a normal range on the follow-up blood test after three months. She reported that her blood tests had repeated this pattern in the last few years. Palpation over her thyroid gland was not significant. The swallowing test was not significant. Palpation over the spine and pelvic region revealed a T5 major subluxation pattern and left anterior sacrum.

Intervention: Orthopedic blocking (single block usage) to correct the left anterior sacrum and adjust T5 and L1 based on functional neurology and Merick system that explains which spinal segment associates which organ. . I used the thump technique by STO over the TP and the side of TP to create a loop to the brain. Digestive enzymes along with adrenal support supplementation were recommended on the initial visit.

Result: The patient came back four weeks after the initial visit and reported her diarrhea had stopped completely and the elimination was normalized. She also reported she was off from sugar products and had no more cravings. Three months later, she came back and reported her cholesterol had dropped by fifty points.

**Case Two:** A thirty-three-year-old Asian female visited our clinic with a chief complaint of chronic neck pain and severe constipation. She stated that she was taking a prescription for her constipation that had started since her infantile period as far as she recalled. She had tried many different kinds of self-remedies such as eating prunes, fibrous fruits, senna tea (Chinese herbal medicine), concentrated baby milk remedy, exercise programs to activate organ systems, and so on; however, she could miss eliminations for a week easily when she skipped these remedies. Then she shifted to over-the-counter medications and prescriptions. She stated it still took her approximately three days to have elimination after she ingested the prescription medication.

Objective findings: Palpation over the spine and pelvic revealed right anterior sacrum and multiple cervical segmental dysfunctions.

Intervention: Orthopedic blocking to correct the right anterior sacrum, T5 and L1 adjustment were rendered on the initial and second adjustments at month intervals. I also activated the ICV (ileocecal valve that is a valve connecting the small intestines and large intestines to control fluid flow as well as elimination) by CMRT (chiropractic manipulative reflex therapy). Cervical stair step procedure was rendered on each visit. On the third visit, she was blocked as Category II.

Results: The patient reported that she went off the prescription after the first visit and off the over-the-counter medication after the second visit. She reported that she was off from all her medications. She still needed to drink Yogi tea for elimination, but was relieved from the cervical pain.

Discussion: According to the American Endocrinology Association, there are approximately twenty-six million people in the United States suffering from thyroid conditions including euthyroid conditions in which a patient exhibits thyroid symptoms without manifestation on the blood test. The case one study is a typical euthyroid condition or borderline hyperthyroid condition.

Regarding sugar cravings, one of the top acupuncturists who has been invited to the White House to treat former presidents and has been invited by various government offices in Asian countries to teach his techniques, stated all addictions come from SI joints articulation. What he does is insert needles and place accu-beads on each ear alternatively with many different combinations. The patient presses those accu-beads lightly to activate and align the SI joints; however, his methodology takes a while to correct SI joint articulation. Dr. De Jarnette stated that a 1/8 inch of block insertion makes a big difference for the correction of SI joint articulation in his manual. Block position adjustment, little by little, is the art of chiropractic. That is the name of the STO manual, *The Art of Chiropractic*, by Dr. M. L. Rees.

Regarding constipation, hard bowel movements create

pressure to the internal wall of the colon, from not only a deficiency of fiber-rich foods, but also the pressure of the hard bowel movement results in diverticulitis in the long term. I observed this is the reason why medications, supplements, or dietary changes do not work all the time.

I believe these fine adjustments for the fine SI joint correction requires the blocking technique.

The acupuncturist also treats patients who get injured by chiropractic manipulation and he asked me to teach the technique I use. Well . . . regulations are different so that I did not teach it, but he knows chiropractic care works more quickly.

Concerning the anatomical structure, the pelvic splanchnic nerve comes out from the S2, S3, and S4 to innervate the colon, kidneys, bladder, and male sexual function. By crossing your legs, it brings the side of the pelvic bone backward. The sacrum bone may compensate by going forward because it is connected by ligaments to create a counterbalance. This is the biomechanics as I explained earlier. This nerve itself controls the colon that may induce thyroid conditions because the colon is associated with immune system. I will explain the mechanism on hearing impairment with this nerve later. In Oriental medicine, the kidneys are supposed to be the major organ to produce energy so that chronic fatigue syndrome can be associated with SI joint misalignment along with kidney function. In Western medicine, the kidney is considered an organ to filter out toxins from your system and one of the causes to control blood pressure by the Angiotensin system along with the liver. This nerve also controls male sexual functions such as erections. Although I did not have the case study of erectile dysfunction (ED), it could be associated with the malposition of the sacrum compressing this nerve that is possible to correct.

The vagus nerve is the spinal afferent nerve (sensory nerve) according to the oncologist, Dr. David Agus, MD; however, this is my professional opinion that this nerve has both afferent (sensory) and efferent (motor) components. The reason I say this is because the thyroid gland is innervated by a branch from the vagus nerve; but, the majority of the vagus nerve is afferent. On the other hand, the majority of the pelvic splanchnic nerve is efferent to control the majority of organs. I do not describe this in detail for the purpose of this book.

Conclusion: In these case reports, the patients' favorable response suggests that SOT single blocking technique along with T5 vertebra and L1 adjustment were directly associated with elimination. Further study is required to determine if other patients with varied presentations might also benefit from SOT blocking procedures and thoracic 5 and lumbar 1 adjustment.

These case studies are the rough draft and framework for my thyroid paper. Neurotransmitters, enzymatic reactions, and immune components related to the colon functions and adrenal stress to secrete stress hormones that cross the blood brain barrier to link with brain receptor sites all kick in to complete my thyroid paper. I was invited by the endocrine association conference at a point; however, the endocrinologist had no clue what I am talking about. As I said earlier, I could be on the side of a crazy person. We need a team made up of all kinds of specialists with different brains working together. Teamwork makes our life much easier.

Some research reported that endometriosis may be caused by crossing the legs. Both female and male reproductive organs are unstable. The female reproductive organs are just connected by a thin membrane to hold its position in the abdominal cavity so that malposition of those reproductive organs are easily induced by postural stress that may result in infertility, miscarriage, premature birth, and so forth. Male reproductive organs are just hanging down outside so it means more exposure to EMW, thermal changes, etc. Check your head position and shoulder levels by looking at mirror. Is your head tilted to one side? Are both shoulders at the same level? Check your neck and feel the muscles around your neck! Is one side tighter than the other side? By crossing your leg, it affects your entire body, affecting the nerve, creating TMJ problems that affect entire cranial motions. Okay, that's enough. Let's move on!

**Incontinence:** A seventy-nine-year-old white female with a chief complaint of incontinence.

Intervention: Similar manner to correct constipation and diarrhea to align the SI joints in a few visits.

Discussion: This patient was under maintenance care, it may take longer depending on the degree of SI joint dysfunction. I don't know how long it holds its position; it may hold for a while, it may come back if you cannot correct your habit, do not cross your legs.

As far as I recall, she did not complain about it for more than a year.

Usually many of my patients came back with a different complaint after a year or a few years. No wonder I lost my business.

Result: Remission of incontinence.

**Arrhythmia: Case One:** A thirty-nine-year-old Asian male who is a runner visited our clinic with a chief complaint of lower back pain. He has a history of lower back pain starting a few years ago from lifting heavy furniture. He did not have any traumatic incidence this time. The physical exam indicated significant irregular pulse rate that he admitted and acknowledged that his father had an irregular heart rate as well.

Intervention: Category III that indicates spinal disc problems in SOT blocking twice a week that reduced his lower back pain approximately 80 to 90 percent so he could attend the twenty kilometer running race that weekend and completed the race without walking. On the third visit, after he went on a long driving vacation, I was going to block him as a Category II that indicates ligament laxity over SI joints in SOT, but I blocked him as III instead of Category II, which created sacrum cup that is terminology used in SOT and located at the sacral foramina. Then, I adjusted the sacral foramina approximately at the level of S2 and S4 on the right.

**Case Two:** A fifty-seven-year-old Asian male came in with entire neck and back pain.

Objective findings: An X-ray revealed major arthritis in his neck and the entire thoracic as of DISH (diffused idiopathic skeletal hyperostosis). Neck motion was significantly reduced in all ranges. Coincidentally, I detected that he had an irregular pulse by auscultation of the heart. I referred him out to his primary doctor who performed an EKG that confirmed an arrhythmia and he was further referred out to a specialist.

Intervention: Category II, III, and orthopedic blocking for the anterior sacrum.

Discussion: I screwed up case one over the blocking positions. Arrhythmia is supposed to be caused by hemisphericity that is a brain imbalance. It is interesting to correct the hemisphericity from the sacrum.

Result: The pulse rate was regulated in both cases. The irregular pulse came back on case two when he came back after three weeks and he admitted he keeps his wallet in his back pocket.

I need to think it over to modify the procedures, but I already have some more ideas.

The following diagram is about the nerve I am talking about. It's all connected from the sacrum to head.

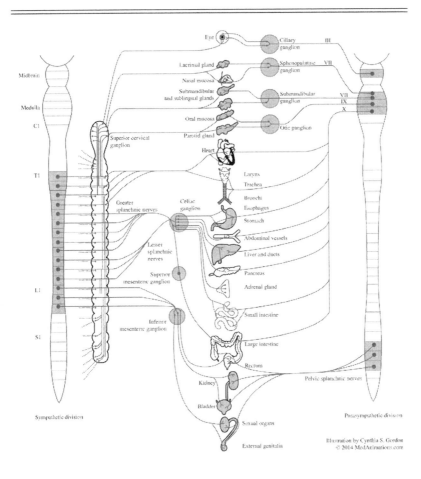

Illustration by Cynthia S. Gordon
© 2014 MedAnimations.com

**Metabolism with radiating pain in the arm:** A fifty-six-year-old Hispanic female visited our clinic with a chief complaint of right neck pain that radiated down into her right entire arm and to the right temporal region. She had injured herself at her work and was under a different chiropractor's care for over ten years. The treating doctor declared her condition had reached a permanent and stationary status after six years. She had an X-ray and MRI that did not reveal any particular abnormality in her neck so that both the treating doctor and the evaluating medical doctor offered the diagnosis as a sprain and strain in her neck.

Objective findings: Palpation revealed a bulged disc at the C5/C6 area on the right. AK doctors call it the "hidden anterior cervical disc" as an MRI exam does not reveal the small disc bulge oftentimes. A majority of regular chiropractors do not palpate the anterior portion of the cervical spine, but the anterior bulged disc is palpable.

Interventions: SOT blocking along with cranial work.

Discussion: This patient also had an additional bonus as she lost twenty pounds in conjunction with digestive enzymes. Why? Nerve interference from the sacrum activated those internal organs and the sympathetic chain at the cervical region linked with a cervical plexus and cranial nerve 11 that innervates the SCM muscles and trapezius muscles on the same side. Compression of the nerve at the sacrum area on the right in this case resulted in the muscle contraction of the SCM that pulled down the mastoid process of the temporal bone causing the TMJ problem. This is a philosophy of SOT about the relationship of the SI joints, the SCM, and the TMJ on the same side, resulting in a tilted head.

Result: The majority of symptoms were resolved in ten visits.

Comments: How can doctors give a diagnosis like this? A sprain/strain does not cause radiating pain in the arm or other regions. Diagnostic tools are not always accurate. More than ten years of the same symptom!? Please investigate! I feel sorry for the patient and the insurance company.

Can you tell how bad a habit it is to cross your legs? If you feel comfortable or more stable by crossing your leg, it is time to see your chiropractor. Many of my patients who quit this habit feel so much relief from the tension from their back and neck. I told you that your body knows what to do. I think the disease process, particularly chronic conditions, are closely linked with the accumulated stress to your system, not only chemical and structural stress, but also mental and emotional stress to your body.

The following diagram is about the nerve bundle in your neck that links with the diagram on the previous page. We need a bigger chart to connect each diagram because every single body part is connected by the nerves.

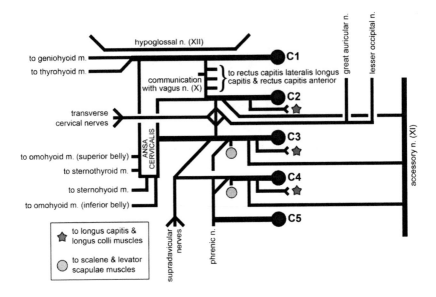

**Uterus Myoma**: A forty-four-year-old Asian female visited our clinic with a chief complaint of lower back pain along with a large tumor on her uterus that made her look about five months pregnant. She had a history of a bad sprain to her right ankle and needed to wear a cast for six months approximately thirty years ago.

Intervention: Category III, II, I blocking and ankle adjustment, more than thirty office visits along with deep breathing exercises at her own expense. Rebirthing, a form of deep breathing exercise along with meditation, for ten sessions or so. She cried over and over in each session.

Discussion: While I was working on the uterus myoma by advanced STO, I could not obtain significant changes; but, I observed significant changes after the deep breathing exercise. I am aware that it was in the newspaper about rebirthing as the rebirther wrapped around a teenage girl to pretend as if she was in a cocoon that resulted in death to the girl. As I said earlier, it all depends on the practitioner's philosophy and belief and every kind of healing has both positive and negative aspects. I never wrap around my patients unless they request to cover up with a blanket to keep warm. Don't be a stereotype! This case study indicates emotional stress affects the physical body. Even though the ankle sprain might not be severe enough as in this case, the patient needed to modify her gait to compensate and it affected her entire structure.

Result: Her tumor and lower back pain were gone!

This patient came back because her insurance company did not pay for the entire chiropractic sessions. She was mad at me because she needed to pay for the remaining balance in spite of her own requests to feel better. It's not easy to make patients happy no matter what we do.

**Right physiological short leg and left anatomical short leg:** A forty-seven-year-old white male visited our clinic with a chief complaint of lower back pain along with TMJ problems. He was under my care for a while and those problems came back repeatedly.

Objective Findings: An X-ray indicated a left anatomical short leg by iliac crest levels. Tape measurement indicated 5mm short on the left.

Intervention: Switched the block position as of left short leg at Category I block position. On the following visit, I blocked him as SB minus. Lastly, I blocked him as Category II.

Discussion: The sacrum position affects leg length. The

gluteus medias as a posterior muscle below T6 and the iliopsoas muscles as anterior muscles contribute significant changes on Category II as of sacrum and pelvic articulation. According to Dr. De Jarnette, we need to perform a stress test on those muscles to determine if there is a shift. Many patients indicate a right physiological leg length difference by traction of the legs; however, application of these muscle stress tests exhibit leg length change. Many of them have a left physiological short leg. Some people notice there is leg length difference by alteration of pants' length or one side of knee is slightly bent at standing position physiological leg length difference often times. Physiological leg length is often caused by pelvic torsion and / or muscle tone imbalance corrected by chiropractic adjustment. Anatiomical short leg is less than 5 percent of the population by shortened leg length by fractured bones or congenital abnormalities of bone growth and etc. It seems there was a shift of those leg lengths after the 90s. Why? I don't really know, but, personal usage of cell phones and computers have spread out dramatically in the past twenty years. More satellites? Increased stress level could be another consideration because everything seems to be speeding up because of our automated systems.

Comments: All chiropractors and other doctors! Please investigate if your patients are coming back with the same complaints over and over. I feel sorry for the patients and insurance companies.

**Hearing Impairment:** Case One: A sixty-five-year-old Asian male with a chief complaint of a gross TMJ problem and hearing loss.

Objective findings: Gross deviation of the right TMJ on the same side as the hearing impairment. Tuning fork application to test any deviation of hearing and air and bone conduction of the sound. No air conduction and no bone conduction on the right ear.

Intervention: The SOT blocking procedure along with TMJ correction, the kidney lift procedure by STO and C4 bilaterally.

Case Two: A twenty-three-year-old Asian male with a cluster phobia. He had a history of head trauma from falling down a staircase twice from top to bottom when he was a child. He had a learning disorder during certain periods of time.

Objective findings: Air conduction on the right was significantly decreased in comparison to the other side. Category II, T12 and T3 subluxation, along with C4.

Discussion: I did not get an audible one when I adjusted his neck, maybe a minor one.

The nerve connection from the sacrum innervates the kidneys and also links with the sympathetic chain to synapse from the segments as T12 is associated with the kidney that is linked with the lung in oriental medicine that coincides with T3. The C4 is also associated with Category II in SOT. Nerve connection through the homologous column from the sacrum through the thoracic region to the cervical plexus resulted in improvement. This procedure required specific neck positions in functional neurology. "Eureka!"

Results: Bone conduction was 70 percent better after the first adjustment in case one. As his tympanic membrane (ear drum) was ruptured, there was no way to get back the air conduction on case one. Air conduction was significantly improved after the first visit in case two.

One of my classmates in the neurology courses stated that she has Meniere's disease, had an SOT blocking procedure and her hearing was improved. Why? It is the same as the "diarrhea and constipation" scenarios. The sympathetic chain coming out from the sacrum links with other cranial nerves at the cervical plexus. In Oriental medicine, kidney function is related to the ear because both of them have similar shapes as kidney beans. I talked to a PhD, a hearing specialist during the flight back to my home country, and he was on the way to lecture about hearing over there. I told him about the concepts of Oriental philosophy about the kidney and ear. He replied that there is a relationship between kidney functions and hearing. He said "Yes! They are related to each other!" I needed his brain to explain further details. What I can think of is that the sympathetic chain comes out from the sacrum, the nerve innervates the kidney and goes upward and connects to the segments I activated from the bottom up. Functional neurologists check the pupils for sympathetic activities; but, I check your butt first if you are under stress or not. It is my opinion that we need to check both ends and both sides of the body if the sacrum is out of place or not because both parasympathetic and sympathetic activities are coming from the sacrum. It's all connected! If you adjust the patients by side posture, particularly the sacrum, you are taking high risks to create further torque over the meningeal system on your patients and increase risks on injuring your own shoulder. Why do we stick to Newton physics? Our science has already shifted to Quantum physics. The force we apply is equivalent to the force we absorb. Be gentle to your patients and to your own body! So many people are afraid of chiropractic because of forceful adjustments; however, our brains perceive signals more by force if we follow the neurological pathways. We need changes.

Probably you already noticed that I am adjusting the nerve connections, not directly to the area of complaint. Usually patients don't know how the body is connected. Western medicine also focuses on each body parts and patients need to travel to each specialist. That's their philosophy about our body and we still need to confirm by scientific measures. If you would wait until the symptom comes up, you are waiting for bigger medical bills and lots of prescriptions that work for the symptoms well and some of you need it. It is your choice. My recommendation is

"Be proactive!"

**HIV:** A fifty-year-old white male with a recent finding of HIV+. He called me on Sunday afternoon while I was working on my taxes. I told him the story that one of my friends had a HIV case in the past whom I had trained how to absorb energy by deep breathing for three years and I adjusted him once. My friend reported to me that his HIV became negative about three months later, and he was under all sorts of investigations at a state university. Then, we went to my office and I adjusted him with advanced STO that is an energy form like one of the case studies in dystonia. I did a follow-up that night and advised him to have another blood test. He reported that the majority of his symptoms were gone after the adjustment, but he called me day and night and told me his immune factor on the blood test was quite high. But, he was told that his blood sample was mishandled so that he needed to have another blood test. He came to my office over and over for additional consultations. I asked him I would charge him for the follow-up visit and consultations. He refused to pay and sent me an email that he would order a restraining order against me. He was gone. Is that the way of "never admit!?" A couple of months later, his friend called me to notify me that he had killed himself. I could not sleep on that night. His friend called me again about a month later and told me that he had killed himself because of a broken heart, financial issues, difficulties in finding jobs, and so on. There was no way to know the result on this case after he was gone; probably I coud not reverse it. We doctors sometimes experience patients who commit suicide due to illness or other personal financial issues. I feel so sorry for the patients, but we cannot solve all of your problems.

Doctors' jobs are not easy, particularly for the people who wait for the last minute and rush into the doctors' office for an emergency. Oftentimes, these patients drain the doctor who has to deal with these patients who can become more demanding, ignoring office hours and are impatient. On the other hand, patients may have problems in finding good doctors, but if you wait until the last minute, it is harder to find a good doctor. American people have so many limitations in trying to select a doctor in this HMO/PPO system on top of it. I also had a problem on collections, particularly men who ran away after one visit or a couple visits. Marketing and advertisement companies ran away after they ran the credit card and found out they did not do any work. Yellow page ads and Better Business Bureau list the names, but are no longer effective. The BBB could be a little better than the yellow pages to check and to look for a good doctor. The insurance system of reducing payments, delaying the payments, threatening patients to reach the settlements and so many marketing calls that I call scavenger calls, so that I did not want to answer the phone and some of you have the habit of hanging up without leaving a message. Discriminations, bias toward chiropractic, "quick and easy" in and out mentality, your understanding about your body, even if I give a good result, the majority of my patients did not refer me to other patients. Once you are done, done with the doctor, which killed my practice and is killing other good doctors. It is also very hard for a minority to get into the American community because of discriminations. That's why my case studies are mainly by Asian people. Many insurance agents do not return the phone calls and they call back right away when my husband call them. Many American people may be desperate for money by losing their jobs and houses. Lawsuits against minor incidences are very violent to me. Some law firms also encourage clients to bring lawsuits against doctors or the side effect of drugs is another litigation. As a result, people do not talk to each other, email communication or text messages and brief conversation resulted in drying out our relationship. It's a huge mess and people are so stressed out now all over the world. Particularly in the countries missing a good leader, I would say the United States is one of the countries in a major crisis, particularly in health care.

I do not want to make judgments and discriminations about others' values, so I do not say SOT/STO is the best. What I observed and what I learned through chiropractic seminars, SOT and STO has so much adjustment tools to work on neurological problems by cranial work, along with sacrum position techniques, direct organ manipulations, and extremity techniques. As a matter of fact, I do neurological tests on patients. The parietal drift test for instance is usually corrected by blocking itself on the first visit. Blind spot tests are also correctable by cranial work. If patients have structural problems, why not try to adjust the structure first. I told you the weird bird is me. I got a big mouth and I poop on your windshield. It's me! I am a chiropractor. I get your nerve! That's my job.

The audible is not always necessary, the key is to create two loops between the brain and other body parts. Sorry! Please forgive my big mouth! But, I love you, all of my fellow chiropractors. I know some of you are much better in some conditions than me; these are my recent findings to share with you as a fellow chiropractor. Please keep up your good work on your patients.

All doctors, not only chiropractors including myself, but also medical doctors, think about what we are doing to our patients and how our patients feel. I am not saying I can cure everything or that I strongly oppose Western medicine. I actually do not cure anyone. I just assist patients to heal by their own healing ability by correcting structure and support nutrition. I accept all kinds of medicine if the patient chooses to maintain their health. I prefer to team up with medical doctors to work on some complicated cases, particularly life-threatening conditions. Patients have the right to choose doctors and treatments so that our job is to secure patients. I also believe patients need to know about their health, their functions, and how much ability they have lost. Many people are not aware of their loss of functions such as smelling or hearing, joint motions, internal organ functions, and so forth before pain or symptoms show up. The scary part of cancer is there is no pain in the early stage so that patients can ignore minor signs if you don't know about your body. Know your body by both scientific measures and functional measures.

I am just asking you, how can we minimize the risk to the patients and avoid lawsuits against doctors? It is not easy to deny what we believe in; however, we sometimes need to think over what kind of risk factors a patient would get. We all learn from mistakes, we all learn from patients as well. We are all human, including doctors, who make mistakes and forget. As far as I understand, the premise of medicine is that doctors should provide the patients' needs at an affordable rate.

Thomas Edison stated that future doctors will treat patients more in the human frame.

I am not saying I am the best, or that I know much more than you. Some of you can do a much better job than I do and know much more than I do in some fields. If you say so, you are focusing on your ego; you have a closed mind and are a discriminator. We share some of the ideas as a friend and a team partner. I am not a straight A doctor so that I still pull out my manual to confirm the procedures in front of my patients sometimes. I think it is better than pretending I know everything I do. Some of you may think I am incompetent. I still need to learn so many things from you, medical doctors, other healthcare professionals, and from patients as well. As I learn, I will find out more and I change it. It's all a learning process. What's next?

# QUICK AND EASY DOES NOT WORK TO MAINTAIN YOUR HEALTH

All sorts of fast food restaurants started in the United States that may represent the culture of this country. It seems that so many things are disposable, including human beings. It is convenient and cheap, Styrofoam, plastic, and so many other items, including cosmetics, are made from oil and many places in the United States do not recycle. I am amazed that there is a long waiting line at the drive-through at fast food restaurants around breakfast, lunch, and dinner time. Many American people do not cook, many of them may not know how. They eat microwavable TV dinners, fried chicken, pizza, hamburgers, and so on. It might be cheaper than cooking for a single person, even for the whole family, and kids love it oftentimes. I see many advertisements, highlights on the top page of magazines on how "quick and easy" it is to lose weight. I heard the magazines are not sold unless we use the headline. We humans love "quick and easy" and I suppose that is the major reason fast food restaurants and electric and electronic appliances for the household are spreading all over the world. It's good for housewives to do other things or work; yet, we need to differentiate the junk food from real food.

I had a patient who was a high school boy with a complaint of fatigue and needed to have a nap after school every day.

He had moved to the United States four or five years before this visit. His mother was concerned about his health because teenagers are usually full of energy. I ran a saliva and urine test to analyze his systems by a computerized lab unit. What I found was that he had major stress on his digestive system as well as his adrenal gland. He was eating fast foods for lunch at school all the time that may have been why he ended up with such fatigue. Luckily enough, he could regain his stamina and could have two part-time jobs and go to the gym after his part-time jobs within a month. I recommended supplements to support his stressed organs. The other case study was on a high school student who sprained his ankle frequently and he was gone after a couple visits. He repeated the ankle sprain so that I advised him and his mother to stay under the care for several visits until I could go into the actual cause. The majority of patients think that pain is the main concern for them. As you read through some case studies in the section "My Report of Findings," the majority of the patients don't really know the major problems causing the pain at the site. The patient's main focus is the pain; however, the descriptions by the patients sometimes mislead health care professionals. It is not easy to find the actual cause oftentimes. Some medical doctors prescribe medication so easily and many of them mask the symptoms so that the patient may end up with so many different kinds of medications. According to a research study by the oncologist, Dr. David Agus, MD, one kind of medication may work for 20 percent of the patients. How about the other 80 percent? If it does not work, medical doctors look for a different kind. That is a struggle for both doctors and patients. Medications used to be prescribed for temporal necessity, but now it seems it is for the rest of their life. Usually you need to increase the dosage and require stronger pills after a while. Why? I suppose the majority of people have difficulty modifying their lifestyles, and keep doing whatever may cause the conditions. I had a patient who is a chemist and works for a pharmaceutical company to formulate medications. He knew what was in it so that he did not want to take the medications. When they moved into a different area, his wife had a little trouble in adapting to the area and saw the doctor who gave her Prozac. His response to his wife was, "Never take the medications!" Our nephew works for a pharmaceutical company and told us the composition of pure medication is 6 percent, the rest of the 94 percent is junk chemicals. No wonder there are so many side effects. People who stay with a poor diet or junk food oftentimes end up taking various prescriptions in mid-life or have multiple surgeries to remove the gall bladder, kidney problems, and develop the endocrine problems. One of our friends had surgery and told us, "That was my eighth surgery on a healthy person!" My mouth dropped. My understanding of a healthy person is that a person does not have surgeries so many times. Another friend was complaining about the price of prescriptions because she needs to take a lot. Both of them were in their mid to late fifties. Although they are functioning to keep up their daily activities, both of them have lots of pain. We sometimes need surgery if the condition is severe enough or we may have major injuries. The question is whether surgery is inevitable or not. Most chronic cases can be avoided depending on how you modify or modulate your diet and activities. The majority of healthcare professionals say, "Eat your food!" it doesn't mean junk food. Food means a good healthy, balanced diet that includes various vegetables, fruits, poultry, fish, nuts, and grains to supply various nutrients. What I am saying is just commonsense. Eating junk food and taking lots of vitamins does not maintain your health. If you keep eating junk food, oftentimes, you are creating your system into a garbage bag. Many of my American patients take a grocery bag full of unnecessary vitamins, and they may not work for them when I do the muscle testing. Muscle testing may require some skills and practice. Some say surrogate muscle testing would be more accurate to avoid the observer's effect. It is your belief system to supply the nutrients. If it works for you, you should feel the difference when taking them. Then, it is worth what you pay for it. If you do not feel the difference, don't waste your money. If you want to do the muscle test to select your supplements, the muscle test does not work for "quick and easy" by online shopping. Consult with a chiropractor, or naturopathic doctor or you may need to go to a natural food store to do it with a friend, family, or a partner. The majority of vitamins and minerals are called supplements to support our diet. Many of the tablet forms of vitamins contain binders and junk chemicals, particularly drugstore name brands. It's cheaper; but, be careful!

A recent study on multivitamins indicates they may increase certain cancer risks. These accumulated stresses to the system could cause various diseases. Many patients say, "It happened quickly!" It's not true . . . The patient experiences the symptoms that show up suddenly. Unless any traumatic event happened such as food poisoning, lifting heavy objects, infections, and so forth, it is not a surprise. I am talking on a daily basis and I am telling myself, too. That's a natural sequence. We people do not pay so much attention to what we do, what we eat, how we use our body. We all screw up our bodies and we are living in such a toxic world. If you don't modify or modulate your lifestyle, the chemical imbalance stays the way it is and goes into the sequence. It is not easy to be disciplined or make good habits for everything that we do. We all try our best . . . don't we? We don't really appreciate what we have until we lose it. One of the water filter companies did so much research on water. Water molecules have two hydrogen atoms and one oxygen atom; it changes its property and characters by how it bonds and can have one million different configurations in an industrial level. Free radicals are one of the risk factors that cause cancer. Tap water in some areas is very acidic. The water filter company reported that children who have not developed enough immunity may get leukemia.

Canned foods and drinks, salad dressings in plastic bottles and sauces in jars, soy milk, any of those products with long expiration dates are loaded with preservatives to make them last longer most likely. Major soda companies are selling filtered water in plastic bottles. Why not buy a water filter machine and fill your own glass or container? Plastic bottles are not safe. It may be cheaper than buying plastic bottled water in the long term. Crystal Geyser water sold at Trader Joe's contains the highest amount of arsenic. Fish may be contaminated with mercury. Heavy metals are hard to remove from our system. Fluoride is added to water that is not a necessary element in our system even though it prevents dental cavities and treats gums. Fluorine is documented to induce cancer. Which do you prefer a cavity or oral cancer? I suppose when our bodies cannot take any more stress to the system, the symptom shows up like stretching out the rubber band that will either fly away or rip. Concerning the foods contaminated with pesticides, preservatives, food colors, and so on, many of them contain unwanted chemicals. Even organic produce can be harmful for some individuals. For instance, eggplant can induce arthritis. Broccoli is supposed to be the most nutritious vegetable; yet, broccoli needs to be heated to neutralize toxins in it. Broccoli and cauliflower can affect thyroid patients. The brown rice diet is supposed be good, but some people cannot eat it. Organic fruits are good, but some people eat a lot and induce an allergic reaction because of too much fructose. The portion you eat is also another factor. It's all good and not good for all and it is all a learning process on each individual. Everything has both good and bad properties.

Pesticides are sprayed from planes over the soil to kill bugs resulting in damaged soil. Strawberries have the highest amount of pesticides. As a consequence, the produce does not have good nutritional value any more. Chickens are grown in the dark so they secrete more growth hormones, are injected and feed hormones to grow to the full-size chicken in a week. Other meat products are similar. We are destroying our earth and our health that is a part of nature by quick and easy shots. Why doesn't the FDA regulate the food industry and require it to put this on labels? We have a right to know how foods are produced, prepared, and genetically manipulated without raising the price of foods. Many young generations in my home country went inland to take care of the soil to grow organic produce because they do not have so many job opportunities due to this automated system. It takes decades to create good soil and to grow trees to create a forest that is the basis to create currents in the ocean that may help to reduce the effects of this global warming. Politics always stinks.

I don't really know if there are any regulations for immune shots in the United States. Some parents can tell the major changes after immune shots to their children and some may develop autism or other neurological conditions because some of the immune shots are derived from mercury. In my home country, we do have regulations to give immune shots to children. We don't give immune shots until they are at least two years old and give it in smaller doses so that parents need to take their kids to a facility to receive shots many times. Doctors or nurses give immune shots, much more in the United States. It saves time for both doctors and parents; however, some kids, and even adults may react more than others. As a matter of fact, some conditions such as polio have a higher incidence after immune shots than the natural occurrence and schools require those immune shots. Again, immune shots have both good and bad aspects. Doctors or nurses can visit daycare centers or preschools to give immune shots gradually. The parents of the children are responsible to give vaccination to his/her own child. Schools should accept children without vaccination. Can we strengthen the immune system of the children? I would suggest probiotic or Air Borne types of supplements during the flu seasons that may help children.

I also recommend trying chiropractic pediatricians or even regular chiropractors first. It is very common that children have atlas subluxation due to strong pressure close enough to cut their spinal cord at the time of delivery. Food allergies also misalign the atlas. Young kids drink milk often and, the most common food allergy is milk according to the Mayo Clinic research. Corn and wheat follow the allergic reaction to milk or dairy products and various food allergies cause headaches, high fevers, digestive issues, and so on. The misalignment of the atlas can cause various problems since the first spinal segment is very close to the brain and ear. Ear infection is very common among young kids that is treatable by chiropractic care along with atlas adjustment.

I have seen so many patients who go downhill quickly from "quick and easy" bandage care. We often take for granted our health and regrets come after if we don't take care of the minor problems. I would say "Good luck on your health and medical bills later!"

Here are some articles for another sample about "quick and easy."

## They're Not Psychotic

Sandra G. Boodman; Kaiser Health News
*washingtonpost.com*
03-14-12

Adriane Fugh-Berman was stunned by the question: Two graduate students who had no symptoms of mental illness wondered if she thought they should take a powerful schizophrenia drug each had been prescribed to treat insomnia.

"It's a total outrage," said Fugh-Berman, a physician who is an associate professor of pharmacology at Georgetown University. "These kids needed some basic sleep [advice], like reducing their intake of caffeine and alcohol, not a highly sedating drug."

Those Georgetown students exemplify a trend that alarms medical experts, policymakers, and patient advocates: the skyrocketing increase in the off-label use of an expensive class of drugs called atypical antipsychotics. Until the past decade these eleven drugs, most approved in the 1990s, had been reserved for the approximately 3 percent of Americans with the most disabling mental illnesses, chiefly schizophrenia and bipolar disorder; more recently a few have been approved to treat severe depression.

But these days atypical antipsychotics—the most popular are Seroquel, Zyprexa and Abilify - are being prescribed by psychiatrists and primary-care doctors to treat a panoply of conditions for which they have not been approved, including anxiety, attention-deficit disorder, sleep difficulties, behavioral problems in toddlers, and dementia. These new drugs account for more than 90 percent of the market and have eclipsed an older generation of antipsychotics. Two recent reports have found that youths in foster care, some less than a year old, are taking more psychotropic drugs than other children, including those with the severest forms of mental illness.

In 2010, antipsychotic drugs racked up more than $16 billion in sales, according to IMS Health, a firm that tracks drug trends for the health-care industry. For the past three years they have ranked near or at the top of the best-selling classes of drugs, outstripping antidepressants and sometimes cholesterol medicines. A study published last year found that off-label antipsychotic prescriptions doubled between 1995 and 2008, from 4.4 million to 9 million. And a recent report by pharmacy benefits manager Medco estimated that the prevalence of the drugs' use among adults ballooned more than 169 percent between 2001 and 2010.

Critics say the popularity of atypical antipsychotics reflects a combination of hype that the expensive medicines, which can cost $500 per month, are safer than the earlier generation of drugs; hope that they will work for a variety of ailments when other treatments have not; and aggressive marketing by drug companies to doctors and patients.

"Antipsychotics are overused, overpriced, and oversold," said Allen Frances, former chair of psychiatry at Duke University School of Medicine, who headed the task force that wrote the DSM-IV, psychiatry's diagnostic bible. While judicious off-label use may be appropriate for those who have not responded to other treatments for, say, severe obsessive-compulsive disorder, Frances said the drugs, which are designed to calm patients and to moderate the hallucinations and delusions of psychosis, are being used "promiscuously, recklessly," often to control behavior and with little regard for their serious side effects. These include major, rapid weight gain—forty pounds is not uncommon - Type 2 diabetes, breast development in boys, irreversible facial tics and, among the elderly, an increased risk of death.

The Latest Fad?

Doctors are allowed to prescribe drugs for unapproved uses, but companies are forbidden to promote them for such purposes. In the past few years, major drug makers have paid more than $2 billion to settle lawsuits brought by states and the federal government alleging illegal marketing; some cases are still being litigated, as are thousands of claims by patients. In 2009, Eli

Lilly and Co. paid the federal government a record $1.4 billion to settle charges that it illegally marketed Zyprexa through, among other things, a "five at five campaign" that urged nursing homes to administer five milligrams of the drug at 5:00 p.m. to induce sleep.

Wayne Blackmon, a psychiatrist and lawyer who teaches at George Washington University Law School, said he commonly sees patients taking more than one antipsychotic, which raises the risk of side effects. Blackmon regards them as the "drugs du jour," too often prescribed for "problems of living. Somehow doctors have gotten it into their heads that this is an acceptable use." Physicians, he said, have a financial incentive to prescribe drugs, widely regarded as a much quicker fix than a time-intensive evaluation and nondrug treatments such as behavior therapy, which might not be covered by insurance.

In a series in the *New York Review of Books* last year, Marcia Angell, former editor in chief of the *New England Journal of Medicine,* argued that the apparent "raging epidemic of mental illness" partly reflects diagnosis creep: the expansion of the elastic boundaries that define mental illnesses to include more people, which enlarges the market for psychiatric drugs.

"You can't push a drug if people don't think they have a disease," said Fugh-Berman, who directs PharmedOut, a Georgetown program that educates doctors about drug marketing and promotion. "How do you normalize the use of antipsychotics? By using key opinion leaders to emphasize their use and through CMEs (continuing medical education) and ghost-written articles in medical journals," which, she said, "affect the whole information stream."

James H. Scully, Jr., medical director of the American Psychiatric Association, sees the situation differently. He agrees that misuse of the drugs is a problem and says that off-label prescribing should be based on some evidence of effectiveness. But Scully suggests that a key factor driving use of the drugs, in addition to "intense marketing and some effectiveness," is the growing number of non-psychiatrists prescribing them. Many lack the expertise and experience necessary to properly diagnose and treat mental health problems, he said. Among psychiatrists, use of antipsychotics is rooted in a desire to heal, according to Scully. "All of the meds we use have their limits. If you're trying to help somebody, you think, 'What else might I be able to do for them?'"

"Since 2005, antipsychotics have carried a black-box warning, the strongest possible, cautioning against their use in elderly patients with dementia, because the drugs increase the risk of death. In 2008, the Food and Drug Administration reiterated its earlier warning, noting that "antipsychotics are not indicated for the treatment of dementia-related psychosis." But experts say such use remains widespread.

In one northern California nursing home in 2006 and 2007, twenty-two residents, many suffering from dementia, were given antipsychotics for the convenience of the staff or because the residents refused to go to the dining room. In some cases the drugs were forcibly injected, state officials said. Three residents died.

A 2011 report by the inspector general of the Department of Health and Human Services found that in a six-month period in 2007, 14 percent of nursing home residents were given antipsychotics. In one case a patient with an undetected urinary-tract infection was given the drugs to control agitation.

"The primary reason is that there's not enough staff," said Toby S. Edelman, senior policy attorney for the Center for Medicare Advocacy, a Washington-based nonprofit group, who recently testified about the problem before the Senate Special Committee on Aging. "If you can't tie people up, you give 'em a drug" she said, referring to restrictions on the use of physical restraints in nursing homes.

Drugs at Eighteen Months

Nursing home residents aren't the only ones gobbling antipsychotics.

Mark E. Helm, a Little Rock pediatrician who was a medical director of Arkansas's Medicaid evidence-based prescription drug program from 2004 to 2010, said he had seen eighteen-month-olds being given potent antipsychotic drugs for bipolar disorder, an illness he said rarely develops before adolescence. Antipsychotics, which he characterized as the fastest-growing and most expensive class of drugs covered by the state's Medicaid program, were typically prescribed to children to control disruptive behavior, which often stemmed from their impoverished, chaotic, or dysfunctional families, Helm said. "Sedation is the key reason these meds get used," he observed.

More than any other factor, experts agree, the explosive growth in the diagnosis of pediatric bipolar disorder has fueled antipsychotic use among children. Between 1994 and 2003, reported diagnoses increased 40-fold, from about 20,000 to approximately 800,000, according to Columbia University researchers.

That diagnosis, popularized by several prominent child psychiatrists in Boston who claimed that extreme irritability, inattention, and mood swings were actually pediatric bipolar disorder that can occur before age two, has undergone a reevaluation in recent years. The reasons include the highly publicized death of a four-year-old girl in Massachusetts, who along with her two young siblings had been taking a cocktail of powerful drugs for several years to treat bipolar disorder; the revelation of more than $1 million in unreported drug company payments to the leading proponent of the diagnosis; and growing doubts about its validity.

Helm said that antipsychotics, which he believes have become more socially acceptable, serve another purpose: as a gateway to mental health services. "To get a child qualified for SSI disability, it is helpful to have a child on a medicine," he said, referring to the federal program that assists families of children who are disabled by illness.

Ask Your Doctor

Psychiatrist David J. Muzina, a national practice leader at pharmacy benefits manager Medco, said he believes direct-to-consumer advertising has helped fuel rising use of the drugs. As former director of the mood disorders center at the Cleveland Clinic, he encountered patients who asked for antipsychotics by name, citing a TV commercial or print ad.

Some states are attempting to rein in their use and cut escalating costs. Texas has announced it will not allow a child younger than three to receive antipsychotics without authorization from the state. Arkansas now requires parents to give informed consent before a child receives an anti-psychotic drug. The federal Centers for Medicare and Medicaid Services announced it is summoning state officials to a meeting this summer to address the use of antipsychotics in foster care. And Sens. Herb Kohl (D-Wis.) and Charles E. Grassley (R-Iowa) introduced legislation that would require doctors who prescribe antipsychotics off-label to nursing home patients to complete forms certifying that they are appropriate.

Medco is asking doctors to document that they have performed diabetes tests in patients taking the drugs. "Our intention here is to get doctors to reexamine prescriptions," Muzina said.

"In the short term, I don't see a change in this trend unless external forces intervene."

health-science@washpost.com.

This article was produced in collaboration with Kaiser Health News. KHN is an editorially independent program of the Henry J. Kaiser Family Foundation, a nonprofit, nonpartisan health-policy research and communication organization not affiliated with Kaiser Permanente.

For more news, or to subscribe to the newspaper, please visit http://www.washingtonpost.com Copyright washingtonpost.com.

Articles featured in Life Extension Daily News are derived from a variety of news sources and are provided as a service by Life Extension. These articles, while of potential interest to readers of Life Extension Daily News, do not necessarily represent the opinions nor constitute the advice of Life Extension.

I know some people need those medications, but some people abuse and take advantage of their privileges and some people may depend on it. You may want to check the locations where a power source is nearby or if you are using a dish network type of cable TV service. Babies and young kids do not have developed brains that may react to the electric power sources. We healthcare professionals need to educate patients as to what kind of risks the medications may create. Functional neurologists talk about these risk factors to screw up your brain by medications. Think it over before it is too late; however, we cannot eliminate all chemical risk factors and electricity or electronic appliances so that they may develop cancer or other diseases, but we cannot live with fear. I am not opposing your choice if you think you need medication or surgery, it's all your choice for your own health. Concerning the risk factors, the questions I come up with, "Who wants to get diseases? Who does not have stress? Who can eliminate all toxins including EMF? Who can live without gravity on top of our own body weight? Who wants to take high risks on health care?" I would say they are all accumulated stresses and not just chemical, but also structural, and emotional stresses as well.

I like "quick and easy," but I learned that it can result in various problems in the long term. Life is tough to cook foods, to deal with people who drive us crazy, to deal with problems, and so on. It is all a learning process; you can change it if you don't like it. Blaming or avoidance of others is easy, but the problem does not go away oftentimes unless you change your lifestyle, diet, how you view things. You, the patients, are the healers.

"Quick and easy" is often violent to nature and nature, which includes your body, does not create any unnecessary waste. Blowers to clean up the backyard are also violent "quick and easy" methods to me and my cat hates it. Some people collect fallen leaves and cover them up with a vinyl sheet to ferment them to produce natural fertilizer. Some people collect leftover food from restaurants to create fertilizer. It's free and you can sell it, rather than waiting for the response from job opportunities or standing on a street with a sign. I heard some street people can collect more than $60,000 a year. It could be a good job; but there is no guarantee.

The Dalai Lama stated, "When you think everything is someone else's fault, you will suffer a lot, when you realize everything springs only from yourself, you will learn both peace and joy." Laughing, crying, depressing, pleasure . . . Unless you go through tough times or hardship, you cannot achieve the accomplishment of real pleasure and it's all yours. That's life.

Because of many lawsuits in the United States, the majority of people, including doctors, are afraid of others. As a result, we cannot trust in people and stop talking to each other. I heard pediatric doctors and OB/GYN doctors are brought into lawsuits, oftentimes. These doctors need to stand by twenty-four hours and have hard jobs. I suppose this insurance system to cut the payment and lawsuits by patients are killing good doctors. Those good doctors are working hard, but the pharmaceutical companies behind the doctors may be screwing up. Think about the side effects on medication on TV commercial. Are patients attacking innocent doctors and killing good doctors? I feel so sorry for those doctors. Life span statistics also indicate that.

A person who appears to be cheerful could be vicious or crying, many marketing representatives are very nice as an example. Some of them just steal money without doing anything or they are so desperate for money. On the other hand, a person who appears to be tough could actually be warm or smiling. My grandmother was a tough woman and she used to call us, "Hey, idiots!" My chemistry teacher was very tough, so I really needed to work hard and the majority of my classmates dropped the class. At that time, I did not like him and the majority of my classmates hated him. When I got a good grade, I appreciated him because he really trained me to study hard. In the article, "Forty-one Things That a Doctor Never Shares with Patients" in Reader's Digest, one doctor stated that a doctor can be judgmental towards the patients sometimes, it could be love telling us why you waited that long to become that serious. When does a patient learn to modify his/her diet, lifestyle and so on? I gave my husband a T-shirt saying, "If you think I got an attitude, you have a perception problem." I used to be very naive and I have become more skeptical to friendly, sweet words these days; it is often a gimmick or fraud marketing. On the other hand, I suppose patients can be judgmental to themselves because they know that they are not taking care of themselves well. We cannot tell ourselves lies about what we are doing, eating, and thinking. We are all busy and forget about taking care of ourselves. We are all stressed out having to deal with so many things, but your body knows and compensates even if you are not in pain. The majority of patients wait until they cannot tolerate the pain, particularly male patients who do not see doctors until it is really bad. We are patient until then and we are not patient when the symptoms come up. It is the natural laws on the downhill slope if we stay on the "quick and easy" oftentimes. When I see my chiropractor, I feel as if I am going to confession because our bodies do not tell lies. The muscle test I described was introduced in England by police officers as a lie detector. Even if you say you are eating only good, organic foods, if your body, your organs are not functioning well, it may not absorb nutrients, or it is not breaking down foods properly. Under the situation, foods inside you could be fermented or putrefied. Usually the inside body temperature is a little higher than your body temperature and we can create our system as a garbage bag to ferment food. My patients who quit maintenance care, or managed care, often go downhill quickly. Some of them develop cancer or precancerous stages in a few years, some of them go into a major distortion of the body.

The majority of patients, not only American people, but also other ethnic groups, stay in traditional ways to seek health care professionals when it is needed, you are a high risk taker and it costs you a lot, later. Considering the increasing rate of cancers, thyroid conditions, and other serious conditions, working on prevention is smarter than waiting for a crisis.

Some companies have already started to hire doctors such as internists, chiropractors, and acupuncturists as company doctors. The HR division can evaluate the doctors and give a bonus if the doctors have good results with the workers. That system may motivate doctors to work even harder. Hire people who stay proactive care; they are the most likely to take less sick leave because they are responsible for their own health.

What we want to do is to secure our health. An annual physical, including a comprehensive blood test including a blood screening test for cancer should be covered 100 percent. Some companies pay the deductible to the employees to cut the insurance premium. If medical expenses were more affordable, probably we wouldn't need high insurance coverage.

What we need is good doctors, not high insurance premiums or very expensive medical charges. That's why I am suggesting you team up with preventative care doctors and medical doctors.

Team up with good doctors in your area and negotiate with them if they can come to your company once a week, or even for a half-day, and rotate the doctors depending on the number of employees.

Why do we pay so much in premiums? To give high bonuses to CEOs of insurance companies? Do you think $1 billion bonus to an insurance CEO is permissible? No!

Get out of the traditional mindset for reactive care!

Think out of the box and do whatever works.

My suggestions in this section:

Keeping up is much easier than catching up!

You need to get out from your traditional mindset for your health and be more proactive.

Observe and learn what kind of habits you have.

Think how much stress you are putting on your body every day by "quick and easy" life styles.

"Quick and easy" health care and losing your body weight are hard on your systems, oftentimes.

That is the reason I am suggesting here how to back up your health.

The following section will cover more about proactive care.

# HEALTH CARE PROVISION

I admire all of the good health care providers including medical doctors, chiropractors, naturopathic doctors, physical therapists, acupuncturists, massage therapists, and so on. You worked hard to achieve your goal to become your profession, no matter what specialty you have. You are helping people to restore their health, to relieve pain, and to alleviate their problems, no matter what method you render. I really admire your passion, enthusiasm, and compassion towards others. We all need good doctors, but this health care system is very outrageous in terms of insurance coverage, premiums, and choices for doctors, hospitals, and so on. In other words, it's CRAP or ripping off each other! Aren't there any other, better ways to manage the healthcare system?

**A Proactive Treatment Plan: Types of care, effects of care, long term effects**
**Bandage Care:** Pain control only; crisis oriented; one to two office visits; does not take care of the cause; most expensive by repeating the same problems.
**Managed Care:** Takes care of the cause; may work for a while; several visits to ten to twenty visits; may not work for other subsequent problems.
**Maintenance Care:** Regular tune-ups to keep your original body parts; avoids major illness/surgeries; preventative care is once a month; least expensive.

**What is your choice to keep your life going?**

I would focus on detoxifying programs more than supplementation because obesity is closely linked with toxicity in your system and I would leave supplementation to the health care professionals.

The companies that provide detox programs I would recommend are:

Biotics Research Cooperation, www.biotics.com.

Transformation Enzyme Co., 1-800-777-1474 The website is www.detoxbylisa.

Colonics to wash out your colon is another option.

Preventative purpose for cancer is Iodoral.

You need to consult with naturopathic doctors, chiropractors, or other health care professionals for those supplements. Many people have allergic reactions to iodine so that I recommend you do an iodine test and consult with your doctor or health care professionals.

You may want to check out www.davidbrownstein.com. He is a medical doctor.

**Immunoal:** Some patients had remission from cancer and some combined with chemotherapy without losing their hair. Dr. Oz also recommends glutathione. Check out www.immunotech.com. You need to consult with naturopathic doctors, chiropractors...to health care professionals."

**My suggestions:**

1. Stop wars to shift the budget to create a National Health Insurance system to cover hospital, dental, vision, chiropractic, naturopathic and acupuncture at an affordable rate, less than $100-$200 for employed workers and $10 for unemployed residents in the U.S. and adjust the rate depending on the income

of the person for all residents in the United States.

2. Freedom of choices of doctors should be included in the Constitution.

3. Create a voting system by the people, not by a small number of people who take advantage of the system or may make a mistake.

4. Cover preventative medicine 100 percent, include twelve office visits per year for people without preexisting conditions. No rejection on preexisting conditions. No deductibles. No prescription insurance; the FDA should regulate the reasonable price for prescriptions. If a person has preexisting condition(s), start with twelve visits with 70 percent coverage before starting twelve 100 percent coverage office visits so it means that the patient needs to see a medical doctor first before starting proactive care for 100 percent coverage to minimize people who take advantage of this system. If a child has complicated cases such as autism, dyslexia, and so on, cover twenty-four office visits. For senior residents, cover eighteen office visits 100 percent first along with medical doctors' care.

5. Cover 100 percent on comprehensive blood work and blood screen tests for cancer by medical doctors every year.

6. Cover medical expenses 70 percent, including prescriptions, and the co-pay would be 30 percent.

7. Create regulations for immune shots to give to children gradually who have not developed their immune system.

8. Import the new technologies for blood screening tests for cancer and the homeopathic types of remedies to treat cancer from Japan.

9. Both preventative care doctors and medical doctors fee schedules may vary depending on the skills and experiences so that the patient needs to pay for the difference, but it should be in an affordable range to avoid draining good doctors. For instance, $120 for a medical doctor visit, $100 for chiropractors, acupuncturists, naturopathic doctors, probably $50 for massage

therapy would be very reasonable.

10. Many insurance companies make doctors slaves, particularly to the HMO. Set up the reasonable rates and the national health care should not cut the payments to the health care providers.

11. Supporting student loans for health care professionals is another consideration to limit an outrageous medical fee schedule by the national insurance system or government.

12. Support any health care professionals, including dentists, for medical equipment that is often very expensive to lower the medical charges. Implant procedures should be covered if they set up the reasonable rate such as $2-3,000. There are so many people missing their teeth.

13. Set emergency hospitals in each city for people who get involved in major injuries, accidents, and illness.

14. Ambulance fees needs to be covered under the insurance.

15. Allow no rejection by the emergency hospitals.

16. For those who choose Western medicine, those proactive care visits can be transferable for some people who need more.

17. Provide more job opportunities for qualification of those transferable proactive care visits at the Social Security Office or welfare office.

In Taiwan, we pay less than $20 premium per month for national health insurance that covers hospital care, dental, vision, chiropractic, and accupuncture care.

In Japan, we pay about $100 by employed workers whose income is less than $100,000, about $200 by employed workers whose income is over $100,000 per year, $10 for unemployed residents.

# WELLNESS CARE PROGRAMS

Approximately 100,000 to 150,000 people die from medical malpractice according to a Harvard study in 1999 and other research. Many people die from complications from infection at hospitals where it has the highest incidence for infection that are not included in the medical malpractice death rate statistics. It has been increasing to 700,000 per year medical malpractice death these days. We human beings are all immortal; yet, it is still very questionable if we can minimize this high incidence of death by medical malpractice and infections. Hospitals used to be cleaned using alcohol, but they are no longer sanitized these days due to budget cuts. Even if many patients are saved by medicine, there is still a very high incidence of malpractice. I hear that many good doctors cannot maintain their private practice and need to hire more billing assistants to collect their bills, on top of high student loans, high malpractice insurance, high stress, along with an increased workload and so forth. There are many "For Lease" signs in medical complexes as well. Some of them share office space to cut down overhead. Usually rent at a medical complex is much higher than a regular professional complex. I suppose good doctors and hospitals are killed by insurance companies after years of training and practice. The HMOs limit the amount of time that doctors can spend with each patient. Many CEOs of insurance companies receive very large bonuses, control the government, bail it out, and so on. Is it permissible?

Once we get used to it, we think that is okay, or we give up
or think that's the way it is. We change the original concept or
sensation. That's adaptation that works both good and bad, but
it is quite dangerous!

It's the same as your body . . . Many people don't know how
many functions they have lost until major pain or symptoms
come up. If you rely on Western medicine in terms of reactive
care, you may be a high risk taker. Various infections are
spreading worldwide, thyroid conditions are soaring worldwide,
the cancer rate is increasing rapidly among the younger
generation worldwide. Why? These conditions are all related to
suppressed immune systems linked with digestive malfunction
and increased stress.

It is so unfortunate that there are so many unethical people,
including professionals. I know there are still many good doctors
and good people. I see many leasing signs in medical complexes
and some cancer centers are closing down because many
insurance companies are cutting the medical payments. Why
do we allow insurance companies to manipulate congressmen?
Many insurance companies do not pay for cancer treatment,
still refuse patients with pre-existing conditions, and increase
premiums without any particular reason. We buy insurance
because we cannot afford the risk of outrageous amounts for
medical charges, and insurance companies still refuse to pay for
some procedures that doctors want to try and some insurance
companies do not pay even if we develop cancer. What is the
purpose of the insurance? There is no warrantee, no security,
no promise, any more. Doctors need to pay high amounts for
student loans, need to buy expensive malpractice insurance, need
to hire more assistants to fight against insurance companies, and
so forth. The education fee is also very expensive in the United
States, but the educational level of the United States is twenty-

fourth in the world. Both parents need to work full-time because it is so hard to raise kids and to pay the mortgage, insurance, schools, and everything else. On the other hand, many CEOs of corporations receive huge salaries and bonuses; the income for one year of a CEO is equivalent to 375 years of income of a regular worker. Who can work for 375 years? If a CEO works in a job position for a day or so, he may understand if the payment for the work is reasonable for the worker or not. Does it motivate the worker or not? Of course, it all depends how we spend our money, it may not be enough, and we all need to learn how to budget our income. Oftentimes, we do not understand quite well unless we experience this. The origin of the word "understanding" means the concept in the brain goes under the body so that we can stand, meaning that experience is the best way to understand. Some workers are laid off just before fifteen years so they cannot receive a pension, if they offer the pension plan, but many companies do not provide pension plans any more. People in their forties have trouble finding new jobs these days after setting up a family and paying the mortgage. These age groups are in their peak time to pay all sorts of expenses. There is no humanity to secure a person's life any more. Life is not an iron man race, particularly in an advanced country. Everything, including utility bills and gas prices, has jumped up. Why do gas prices increase in the summer time? It seems a money game. As a human, we are all born to live, to secure our lives, and to be happy. New technologies are supposed to make our life easier. No! It makes it more difficult to get a job and requires a higher education these days, more than any past generations. Computers worldwide are connected and control about 70 percent of the stock market; a minor flash crash has occurred hundreds of times after the major flash crash a few years ago. Some economists predict about 50 percent of white collar jobs will be eliminated by this automated system in ten years. I suppose agriculture in the future will have lots of potential for job growth.

Human history could be a history of wars. Religious revolutions happened in four hundred year cycles; two thousand years is another bigger cycle; colonization, independence of those colonies, including this country, resulted in the current countries in the world. Civil wars happen in African countries, immigrants from those countries move into some of the European countries and are attributing to the economic and population problems in some of these countries now. After the atomic bombings in Hiroshima and Nagasaki in 1945, we learned the atomic bombs kill not only people, but also the land. Yet, we still have enough atomic bombs to destroy the earth thirty-six times or more. We have shifted from an atomic war to a genetic war these days. There is a rumor that HIV was created to kill certain populations, targeting gay communities, prostitutes, and drug abusers, although it is said it came from African monkeys. SARS has spread across populated areas in Asian countries for a while. There are specific neurological disorders in African countries with unknown causes, and there is a rumor that possibly some countries are doing human experiments over there. Russia and the United States have advanced research and technologies in genetics. Yeah, it's a rumor . . .

Since the beginning of the twentieth century, the majority of wars were initiated by this country except for WW II. There is a rumor that there was a plan to make the Japanese attack Pearl Harbor by refusing trade business and by analyzing Japanese psychology. The 9/11 terrorist attack by Al Qaeda killed so many innocent people in the World Trade Center buildings. There was a discussion about this event in Jesse Ventura's talk show to debate about US politics on TV in September, 2012. There is a rumor that the pilot must have had very high skills like a top gun pilot to target the building to collapse it in one shot at the right angle, not by the skills for regular commercial plane pilots. There were so many hijackings after the 70s that they created a system to control planes from the ground. The World Trade Center buildings were not on the edge of the Hudson River, they were in the center of other skyscrapers. How was it so accurate? My husband got bird droppings on the top of his head through the open moon roof while he was driving on the freeway. I was next to him and laughed so hard when that happened. The bird was so accurate, like a top gun pilot. Yeah, there is a top gun bird. Then, the war started in 2003 while George Bush Jr. was president. So many innocent people, including the young US soldiers, were killed outside of this country. If we kill a person, it is a crime in a normal life, but we are supposed to kill people during a war. It is very contradictory and many veterans suffer from post-traumatic stress syndrome and may not be able to recover from the trauma for the rest of their lives. Those veterans still need to come back to a regular lifestyle. People have trouble adapting from those extreme situations to a regular lifestyle because it may destroy a person mentally, morally, and their personality. Parents in Vietnam dumped their babies because of severe deformities caused by the Agent Orange bombs; Vietnam War veterans stand on the street for food, money, or jobs. The war is not over for these people. We, US soldiers, are killing millions of innocent people in those countries. The United Nations limited bombs harmful to human bodies and human experiments on hostages; yet, war itself is to kill each other.

The economy in this country has been dependent on the wars because we have a strong defense system. The history of this country is a sequence of wars since the very beginning: to conquer the land from the American Indians, to get independence from England, France, and Spain, fighting over freedom and human rights that became the Constitution of this country. The former President Nixon approved the HMO system. The first question he asked was, "Is it more profitable?" We lost our president who had become a puppet for oil companies, insurance companies, and other major corporations. It is getting harder and harder to achieve the American dreams due to this capitalism. It is a big money game, particularly after the 80s.

The war inside this country does not stop at an individual level, to fight to keep their houses, jobs, and so forth. Civil wars are happening in African countries, economic crisis is affecting European countries and many Asian countries except for China. People are fighting over getting their jobs and houses against the dogmatic leader. It does not make much difference what is happening in this advanced country. I know we have been missing good leaders worldwide. No matter who becomes the president, he will be manipulated and be a puppet. It seems that so many industries in this capitalism are in the money games. We observed how Obama changed his appearance, fading so quickly, and changing his propagandas. I saw a greeting card with George Bush Jr.'s picture in front of the national flag, saying, "I really fucked this country, thank you for blaming the black guy!"

I believe in the quote by the former President Lincoln, " Government of the people, by the people, for the people, shall not perish from the Earth.
from "Brainy quote"
Abraham Lincoln

I also support the quote by J.F. Kennedy, " My fellow Americans, ask not what your country can do for you, ask what you can do for your country.
From "Brainy Quote"

John F. Kennedy

Michael Moore created a movie, *Sicko*, criticizing the health insurance system in this country and comparing it to the health insurance systems in other countries. It is quite interesting to watch how other countries are working on health care.

My suggestions for this section are:

1. Start proactive care as soon as possible by alternative health care professionals whatever your choice would be.

2. Team up with your medical doctors and alternative care doctors to make your life easier and to minimize the lawsuits against doctors.

3. Call your congressman and tell him/her about your ideas. If he/she does not represent your opinion, kick out the AH, never vote for him/her again.

4. The term of a congressman should be limited to four years like a president, eight years would be the maximum.

5. Create committees for those politicians, state governers and union people who take advantage of their privileges. Assign penalties such as a big fine in each state and to create more job opportunities for people under IRS provisions.

6. Increase the tax rate for CEOs of major corporations up to 40-50 percent to bring in more budgets to support the national health insurance system and get out of $17 trillion in debt is another option.

Your voice should be heard.

You and your family need to be protected.

We are the people responsible for the changes.

Team up with other people whom you can trust.

Get united with your family, co-workers, community, and associations you belong to which make your life much easier.

Those are the meanings of the Constitution of this country

and the meaning of the country, aren't they?

Medical doctors are starting to talk more about nutrition and there are more natural vitamins and exercise programs these days. Dr. Oz is on TV talking about preventions. I admire Dr. Oz and Life extension doctors and their knowledge; yet, how can regular people keep up with those vitamins and supplements? Many supplements that are supposed to work for various conditions are getting more expensive for a one month supply; it often comes up over $100-200 for one person per month. Even if it appears to be working initially, I can tell the difference if they change the formula oftentimes. Dr. Oz recommends miso soup, I wonder if he knows many Japanese soup stocks and other foods contain MSG, some modified to di-sodium glutamate meaning they have added one more sodium atom to MSG. Many Japanese restaurants use those soup stocks. Some individuals react to MSG right away, particularly instant miso soup. Read the label!

I have tried some other supplements that Dr. Oz recommends that did not work for me. I don't go by what he says; I go by how I feel. If we analyze what we eat all the time, we cannot enjoy our food, choose your food for that moment and enjoy it!

We all need blood work, urine tests, ultrasound, endoscopic exams, X-rays, and so on to check our health for necessity. Many of my patients are not getting these annual physical exams because of this insurance system with its high deductibles. In some other countries, each city created networks with doctors or facilities to provide physical exams annually for the residents at very low rates such as $5-$10 for some medical tests. Sometimes, cities, states, or countries own the hospitals along with university hospitals, private hospitals, and so on. People may move to those cities for more security; usually those cities have a little higher tax. There are so many different ways we can create and there are some books about insurance systems in other countries.

My husband read some of the books about insurance systems in other countries that changed his views about healthcare. The United States is a rare country, in not providing national health insurance like other advanced countries. Yet, working on preventive medicine is more cost effective as is doing annual exams by medical doctors. What is preventative medicine? I think any alternative medicine can be preventative, including massage, particularly chiropractic because the musculoskeletal system is the frame of the body and we bear postural stress to the joints all the time on top of gravity. The majority of chronic conditions are the consequence of stress to the organ systems and skeletal system that affects joint structures, including the spine. Active kids may fall down and hit their heads or get injured often. My mother always needed to keep a good first aid kit while we were growing up. Who does not fall when we start walking? Who does not sprain their ankle sometime in their life? Who can follow the strict diet or nutritional program their entire life? Those micro shifts of the joints can result in bigger problems because your body needs to compensate and they manifest as major or more serious problems later in your life.

There may be a miracle healer to cure all kinds of conditions instantly. I saw psychic surgery on TV a long time ago. One of my classmates told me his grandmother went to the Philippines to receive psychic surgery to remove her brain tumor. I also heard some people who were trained by the psychic surgeon in Philippine are training the method to health care professionals and healers in the San Francisco Bay area.

Some trained healers and gifted healers can remove tumors and reverse other conditions. There are not many gifted healers, but I hear more and more people engage in energetic healing among chiropractors, among acupuncturists, and massage therapists. Reiki masters and craniosacral practitioners are not necessarily among those health care professionals; but, they do a great job and some of them even work on remote healing.

There are some healers in the book, *Call of Sedona*, by Ichi Lee utilizing Dahn yoga. I went to the yoga center in Sedona, Arizona to investigate. I don't think they are medically trained healers and some patients may experience adverse effects during the healing process. The website always gives pros and cons and we cannot go by that. If you have some medical conditions you are concerned about, team up with your medical professionals before you bring it to a lawsuit. As I said earlier, any healthcare procedure has both positive and negative effects. They are all very nice people who treat others as a human being with respect. I believe yoga is a good exercise and it was fun!

Biofeedback and simple visualization can be utilized for self-healing and it can even remove tumors! Some cases are supported scientifically by pre- and post-MRI exams. There are many different styles of healing. Nothing is wrong with it.

I am not saying I am right and I am not saying this is the best way. I am just suggesting to you how we can change this system to provide better medical support for you and your family, and your voice needs to be heard.

Albert Einstein stated that, "Insanity: doing the same thing over and over again and expecting different results.

"We all do the same thing over and over, but we sometimes stop and think differently when exposed to different views. Travelling to other countries and living in another country are completely different things. Talk to other people who are from a different country. They have different systems and different views. So many people in other countries are anti-United States and the United States is only the country not to incorporate with other countries to prevent this global warming to save the earth and is still attacking other countries for oil. There are still some areas that do not recycle. Is overpopulation a major cause of this global warming? Approximately 80 percent of the world's populations are living on the coast and that could be the major problem. I believe the population of the earth has already hit 7 billion in 2012. If we keep on destroying the earth, we may not supply enough food, and there are many people who live on the food stamps in the United States. We may have wars over water if we stay with our traditions to keep lawns in our back and front yards. I would create a Zen garden with stones for no maintenance. I know myself well and admit I am lazy. Some areas already have shortages of water. *Mutant Messenger* is a good book to read about the water shortage and the Aborigines in Australia who set up regulations not to have kids any more. There is no border in the nature, air, oceans, and lands. We, human beings, created borders because of our egos and desire for profits. There are some people who make a profit from wars and may control populations; however, the profit is not for regular people who go to war, for their family, not for the people involved in the war in the area. We are the people living in this country allowing the government to keep doing this. We are the people to stay the "quick and easy" way by not recycling so many things. We are the people who have a power if we get united. Why do we let small numbers of people manipulate our president and squeeze our lives? What we learned from Hitler is to tell people a big lie. I don't believe in whatever your religion is unless you keep your promises or if you are taking advantage of others and privileges. We all have patriotism, we all have emotional attachment to our own families, friends, community, associations, the society we belong to; however, we create discriminations toward the others if we think this is the best, or this is the only way to do it. There are various other ways to do it, that's why we have so many people. Discriminations do not go away if we deny other's values. *The Help* is a movie about discrimination. I wonder if we are treating others like humans. The state of California went to almost bankruptcy because they are dependent on the Mexican people's labor. Mexican people claimed so many work comp cases that many companies needed to pay so much work comp insurance on top of health insurance that it resulted in squeezing their budget to run their businesses, particularly in small business owners. Insurance companies are threatening patients to reach settlements very quickly, asking for secondary insurance, cutting the payment to the doctors and so on. I know some, maybe many, of the patients and doctors are taking advantage of the system. Yet, insurance companies are not treating patients and doctors as a human frame oftentimes. What a mess as a result!

I don't blame Obama, George Bush, or other former presidents. I feel rather sorry for them being under so much pressure from the people who manipulate them. Money can make a person different. Some of the US presidents were killed . . . What do you do if someone tells you, "Do you want multi-billions and can walk away if you do what I say? Otherwise, you will lose your life." The majority of humans are afraid of death; yet, threatening the president to screw up the whole country is not permissible. As far as I have observed, I don't think this system works no matter who becomes the president as long as the people behind the president manipulate our president. I would say that most of countries worldwide have lost their good leaders; that's why civil wars in different counties are occurring. People in Greece under the major economic crisis complain that they cannot afford to buy meats and question why they have to pay the debts when the government screwed up? I would say the voting system by us may work better. The majority would win. I am a Democrat!

I believe this is the year to say "No!" and this is the year to get united. The rich become richer, the poor become poorer. Of course, we need to think over why we get sick, why we get poorer, why we are stressed out. We tend to look for answers outside, but usually we have the answers within ourselves.

# SCIENCE IS A MYSTERY

Science changes all the time. When a new idea is discovered, what we believed in today can be a completely wrong concept tomorrow. For instance, the earth used to be thought of as flat, but we found that the earth is a sphere. I found out there are some people who still believe it is flat. Yes, it appears to be flat if we stand in the middle of the field. It all depends on how we see it. It used to be believed that water was neutral in pH, but we found it can be alkaline or acidic. A Japanese scientist, Dr. Masaru Emoto, found water crystallizes by application of human intention. He claimed the oil spill in the Gulf of Mexico was caused by anger of U.S. citizens. You may want to watch a movie, *What the Bleep Are We Talking About?*

Dr. Andrew Weil was on the top page of *Time* magazine to pray for the patient.

Our brain emitts brain waves that have very high energy. Our intentions, thoughts and emotion are all forms of energy. If we emit brain waves as of good intention, it will create different wave patterns. Healers and doctors can utilize the brain waves for healing and some of them are using as a prayer.

Praying has healing effects. A Harvard study also indicated that meditation can result in the thickness of the cortex. The human brain emits brain waves that are measurable, alpha, delta, theta that are all very low frequency meaning very high energy. The scientist who trained a psychic to bend a spoon measured the frequency of the beams coming out from the outer space concluded they were 8Hz, about the same frequency as our alpha brain waves that ranges from 8-13 Hz. The lower the frequency, the higher the energy it becomes. A good example is AM radio waves that are KHz that travel further than FM radio waves that are MHz that have 1,000 times more waves per second. We are talking about invisible waves that exist and are measurable. Even if we watch one channel on TV, or listen to one radio station, can you deny there are so many different waves for the different TV stations or other radio stations that are emitting the waves at the same time? You just don't tune in or focus on them. We are all bombarded by these waves that are not visible or perceivable from satellites for telecommunications, for TV, for weather, for radio, and so on for twenty-four hours a day, seven days a week.

The British scientist, Alfred Rupert Sheldrake, published, *New Science of Life,* about the effect of brain waves and telepathic communications. They did experiments by broadcasting images on TV, and the distant people would receive the same images without watching the images on TV. Japanese scientists did an experiment on monkeys by feeding sweet potatoes to wild monkeys on the beach. A young female monkey started to rinse the potato in the seawater and the other monkeys followed. These monkeys learned rinsing the sweet potatoes in the seawater that took off the sand and even seasoned them with sea salt. They liked it and more and more monkeys started to do that. When it reached a certain number of monkeys doing this, a distant monkey started to do the same thing without any contact communication between the groups. The experiment was done among by regular people like us, not by psychics in England. These wild monkeys were all normal monkeys. You may want to check out the website www.brucelipton.com. Dr. Bruce Lipton is a scientist in California, and a professor at Stanford University working on these kinds of concepts and wrote many books. He was talking about how the mind will change the stem cells in his newsletter on his website. It is quite an interesting study. Anyway, the key is we need to hit certain numbers to get the effects. You could be the starting person (the monkey) to achieve your goal or you could be the last person to affect others in the distance. The larger the numbers of people, the more powerful the effect we can achieve. We humans can learn and grow and computers are catching up to learn. We still don't know so many things outside of our world. Spaceships land on Mars and linear accelerators are trying to find out if there is a faster speed than light. Scientists and doctors are working hard to find out the causes of various diseases. This century is supposed to advance to knowing more about the human brain. By watching the Olympic Games in London, I was thinking, what is the difference between humans and computers or machines? We can swim, we can jump, we can do so many other things, and we still have a lot more possibilities. That's how we have been developing and created the current cultivation. Nothing is wrong with it. It all depends on how we use the technologies. The major difference between a computer and human is we have a physical body, emotions, and our minds. The most important things are the invisible parts of humanity, to think of others, to trust, to love. If we cannot think of others, a person becomes closer to being an object as he or she loses humanity. There are so many controversial issues and many of them are not easy to make decisions, particularly when we make a decision on human lives. Religions, ethics, morals all come together. Japan is the only country to suffer an atomic bomb destruction, (the United States could be included if we counted the atomic bomb experiments in Nevada) and it has been sixty-nine years since the bombing. I found out the average age of survivors from the atomic bombs is around seventy-nine years in Japan. Some of them saw their family members burned up instantly right in front of them. Windows broke and the shattered glass stabbed them all over their bodies instantly. Houses were burned down instantly. Over 170,000 people were killed instantly. There are still many victims surviving after sixty-nine years in Hiroshima and Nagasaki. I suppose those people have a mission to assert to end the usage of atomic bombs and they are working on their missions. In March 2011, a major earthquake hit the northeast side of the main island in Japan. The tsunami wiped out many small towns and all electricity was blacked out so that it resulted in a nuclear plant explosion in Fukushima. Radiation is not visible and we know it induces cancer after thirty or forty years. Arizona has the highest incidence of cancer in the United States because they had sparkles of radiation from the atomic bomb experiments in Nevada. We are bombarded by radiation, now. When we fly, we are exposed to radiation, particularly on international flights as they fly higher to save fuels these days. We have destroyed ozone layers so that we are exposed to radiation more than before. We cannot get away from it on a daily basis. The question is if radiation is the major cause of cancer or not. I suppose all sorts of diseases are caused by multi-factors, not only a chemical imbalance, but also radiation exposure, emotional or mental stress, and structural imbalance. It's all there and it takes years and decades to manifest the symptoms, although we use radiation for medical purposes to examine patients and to treat them. One of the *forty-one things that a doctor never tells the patients,* one doctor talked about why doctors send out the arthritis patients for an MRI that costs much more than X-rays. I suppose some doctor may want to charge more, some of them may protect patients from radiation. Some of my patients are afraid of radiation in spite of watching TV for hours and frequent air travel. There is a procedure on how to eliminate radiation from your body in STO. Some of the procedures in Western medicine are invasive and have negative aspects. Not only Western medicine, acupuncture may cause capillaries to break down and they used to use non-disposable needles (I believe they use disposable needles only, now). Chiropractic has negative effects such as death by neck manipulations, stroke, bone fracture, and so on; however, some research indicates the rate to induce stroke by chiropractic neck manipulation is 1 out of 5.8 million, much less incidence of problems in comparison to medical malpractice. I don't know how often a chiropractor causes a fracture. It all depends on each doctor's philosophy and application of the techniques. I would say any kind of medicine, including massage therapy, has risk factors because muscle fibers are innervated by the largest nerve fibers to activate the brain and die first. The question is how much risk a patient can take. Probably you already know that cancers or other complicated diseases do not cause pain in the early stages and minor symptoms may have hidden major problems. One of my friends lost her husband from a massive heart attack in five days after he was told his blood test result indicated he had perfect health. I had a patient with severe ataxia. She visited a doctor who did MRI exams that did not indicate any significant findings. She is from my home country so that she went back there and had comprehensive medical exams at one of the top university hospitals because she was concerned over the medical fees in the United States. She spent a few weeks to complete the exams at the hospital. The doctors could not find any significant abnormality. What can a patient do? What can a doctor do? I suspected Frederick's ataxia, but there was no way to confirm it. She could walk and run after a while. She is from a very wealthy family over there, but she had major problems in her marriages over and over. In my case in the introduction is a typical spinal cord tumor scenario that did not show up in any scientific exams except for an elevated protein in the CSF. I was drinking several cups of coffee around that time and I found some research indicated excessive intake of coffee may result in spinal cord tumors. I was so lucky to have met Dr. M. L. Rees and had a post-MRI. After the publication of the effect of coffee to prevent diabetes, many people drink coffee even more. I wonder how much money Starbucks spent for this kind of promotion on its rapid growth worldwide. Starbucks coffee contains more than ten times higher the amount of caffeine for daily recommended values in a tall cup. One cup of coffee is eight ounces, a tall cup size, not a grande cup size. Dr. Oz is talking about green coffee beans to lose weight these days. Science always changes. It is hard to keep up with it.

I also heard there were two kids in the family born without brains; both were very smart and survived until fifteen years old. It is very hard to understand how these kids could survive for fifteen years without brains by the current science. I suppose the spiritual body part and spiritually caused problems do not show up on the scientific exams oftentimes. I will describe why it happens in the next section.

# SPIRIT, MIND, AND BODY

W e are all in the process of development and growth, not only technologies, but also our own humanity and spirituality. The key is if we are open for better changes or not. My husband said, "A mind is like a parachute, it only works when it is open."

Some say this is the end of world. Some say this is the end of a cycle of the Mayan calendar. I believe in the end of the cycle so it means the beginning of another new cycle after 2012. We have been creating materials to cultivate and develop so many materials, mostly something visible. Now, we are talking about something invisible. Although we talk about something visible, we cannot deny there is nothing when we cannot see it which is the same as the concept of the existence of God. If we deny something is invisible, it is coming from there is or not on the premise of existence. There are more and more psychic people who perceive something we cannot see. Silvia Brown is one of the well-known psychics on TV. Some talk about ghosts, spirits whatever you call them. Some people may feel, see, or glimpse spirits out of the corner of their eyes. There are many horror movies, story of ghosts, and spirits, like the *Sixth Sense, Ghost, Poltergeist* and so on. Some empirical psychiatrists, a Yale University graduate started to talk about past lives. Many of his patients went back to their past lives through hypnosis. Those patients could visualize their past lives vividly or feel the sensations that they had experienced in their past lives. Some may go through spiritual experiences, oftentimes by near death experiences, and some project their astral body, spiritual body, soul, whatever you call them, and watch their own physical bodies. Dr. Elizabeth Kublar Ross is a pioneer who has studied death and found out there is a three ounce difference in body weight after the spiritual body has left the physical body. There are so many scientifically unexplained phenomena. Some scientists tried to explain the mechanism of acupuncture or meridians, but meridian points are not visible, not identifiable by physical eyes, but, it exists and has a history of over four thousand year.

The Chinese talk about the energy flow of the house called "Feng Shui." It is supposed to create a good energy flow inside the house, as the arrangement of rooms and construction of the house itself could be critical. Have you heard some weird stories about houses? People who live in a certain house may experience tragedies such as murder, kidnapping, personal bankruptcy, illness, divorce, and so on. It's all about the energy. There are certainly energy flows inside and outside a house. Indians talk about chakras, Koreans started to talk about life particles and the brain particles of the energy flow inside our bodies. Japanese people talk about mind effect over the physical body in Zen philosophy and the emotional effects over water. Sixty to seventy percent of our human bodies are water. Think about the word, e-motion, where e stands for energy so that emotion is the motion of the energy. It is not visible, but we feel it. My husband says, "I feel it right here!" as he points to his lower back when we have a fight. That's the location of the sympathetic nerve, the "fight or flight" nerve and will cause muscle contractions. It is all matters, energy! When somebody changes his or her attitude, we say, "What's the matter?" Yes! It's all energy. Einstein's theory of relativity, E=mc² applies. He also stated that science should merge with religion (which I would include medicine as a belief system.)

Some say each organ associates with specific emotions. For instance, the kidneys are known to be a female organ representing fear, anxiety, or worries. The liver and heart are known to be a male organ representing anger. Some researchers say that cancer is associated with anger and guilt. Loneliness may suppress immunity and particularly white males cannot survive long term alone in old age which is the statistic I learned in geriatric class. Cancer patients also do not laugh and talk a lot for a long period of time. Those emotional factors are not considered well in Western medicine, but it contributes to developing diseases.

Other researcher stated that our life is governed by approximately 90 percent spiritual, 9 percent mental and emotional, and 1 percent physical. Another researcher stated it is 100 percent spiritual, 100 percent mental, and 100 percent physical. It all depends on where we focus, it all becomes 100 percent.

In one of the *Indiana Jones* movies, Indiana Jones traveled to a place where people practice voodoo. The human psyche can be concentrated as much as a master of martial art can move a person fifty yards away by hand motion without ever touching or can make a person suffocate or choke. The universal rule applies any way no matter what . . . The rule is what we give is what we get. The rule of karma. It is to balance the force or energy. Steve Jobs used to be the CEO of Apple computer and he was really harsh to the workers. His physical body could have been affected by negative thoughts, his own attitude, and by the people around him. Spiritual, mental, emotional, and physical are all energy, no matter what it is. It just changes the form and everything is vibrating to determine the form.

Christianity indicates that it is harder for rich people to go to heaven than for a camel to go through the eye of a needle. Since we do not recall the memory of our past lives, we cannot really tell what the balance is in this present life. One percent of rich people in the U.S. who own 40 percent of the wealth may not be able to go to heaven. Look at the Kennedy family; they have had one tragedy after another. Money cannot buy good luck, health, or real happiness.

Helen Keller who created sign language was encouraged by the Japanese novelist who was also a blind person. He founded modern Japanese novels and wrote hundreds of books. Helen Keller then visited Japan before and after World War II to contribute to the Japanese people as a return. She stated that the greatest pleasure as a human is to contribute to others. Physical impairment is inconvenient; however, it does not make any difference on the dignity of the human being. It all depends on how each individual contributes to the society. Everyone is supported by so many people to live. We need farmers who produce the products we eat. We need constructors to build a house. We need plumbers for the water supply, we need electricians, we need musicians, all different kinds of people, and we are supported by these people to live as long as we live in a society no matter where you are. We are all engaged in somehow and somewhat with people. Our brain is constantly working to regulate our systems no matter if you are aware of it or not. The major question is how we use our brain, how we use our heart, how we use our hands. Our brain circuit makes a figure eight horizontally so that it is like the symbol of infinity in math. Your brain is constantly operating in the circuit of the infinity symbol. You have the power to make changes in your life. Use your brain, heart, and hands to move towards the right direction to live. The word live is spelled L, I, V, E, if we use our power or force in the right direction. If you use your brain, heart, and hands in the wrong direction, it becomes E, V, I, L. No matter what race you are, no matter what religion you believe in, no matter what kind of career you have, you are connected with so many different people and God to live. As long as we have life, as long as we breathe, we are connected to God. The author of *Conversations with God,* Neale David Walsch, told God, "Happiness is nowhere!" God replied to him, "You need to put a space between the w and h as Happiness is Now Here!" That's why we call now the present. Life is a gift or present from God. Probably many of you know the tale, "Footprint." A man walking on the beach found there were always two pairs of footprints; he could not find out the other pair of footprints when he was in trouble and he found another pair of footprints after he went through the trouble. He asked God, "Why didn't you help me while I was in trouble?" God replied to him, "I was with you; I carried you at that time."

No matter what culture, religion, or belief you have, we are coming from one source and maker, God, the Lord, whatever you call it. I would say if you are connected to the source, with faith within your heart, it will bring you health, luck, and happiness because what God gives us is our life and love. The creation in nature, our mother nature, sky, oceans, and lands have no borderlines. We, human beings, created the borderlines because of our greediness along with our ego and repeated wars and conflicts. The air you are breathing is the same air people in Asia, South America, Africa, and Europe are breathing. The water levels of the oceans are rising around the world which are also connected. Does nature judge you? No, if we emit positive vibrations by positive thinking, positive creations, positive attitudes, it will come back to you. Negative thinking, negative creations, or negative attitudes will abuse your spirituality and attributes negativity in your life. Nature does not judge you, but you judge yourself by your own thinking, creations, and attitudes. Fear, for instance, would be negative, but nature provides whatever you visualize, think, and feel and it becomes real. The majority of cancer survivors are afraid of a reoccurrence of the cancer. Usually, people who do not want to change their lifestyles, diet, or work on prevention are afraid of reoccurrence. If we don't learn the lessons, we need to come back again to the school of life. We, Asians, call this reincarnation. I am excited that some Oriental philosophy is accepted and merging with Western culture. That is the balance force, or the rules of karma. Ying and yang! If you are angry, you may be feeling that you lack power to control somebody or something. Control over somebody is more focused on your ego, we can discuss and create consensus that would promote synergy. There is always an opposing force, emotions and thoughts to balance. The opposite emotion of fear is excitement. When we encounter new things, we may be afraid or we may get excited. We all need to forgive others and forget the past as no one can live in the past. The past, present, and future are all connected through the pathways of our life. Only what you can control is the present by changing your viewpoint. There is no time in the universe; we created time as a convenience. Unless we forgive ourselves to forgive others, we create negativity. The human mind and emotions have not changed for years and decades, sometimes for an entire life. It all depends on what aspect you are focusing on. The words forgive and forget are spelled for give and for get. Interestingly enough, those words are our gain. Forgive is to love ourselves and others. That's how I understand what the Dalai Lama means.

The majority of other countries are not attacking the other countries except for some Palestinian areas. If we focus on our egos, fights and wars will never end. We, all human beings, can turn negativity to positivity if we learn from our mistakes and if we use our power to the right directions. The power is not to have control over others; the power is to support others. Weapons are a force to gain control over others. We can have different ways to solve our problems. Don't let a small number of people screw up your life.

Can you use your heart to help others?

Can you help others create a new voting system to have a national health insurance system in the United States?

Can you talk to your friends, family, or co-workers about this idea to protect you and your beloved ones?

What I am saying could be wrong, that's why I am telling you that your voice needs to be heard. I just feel so sorry for my fellow American people that you pay taxes and high insurance without security. I am sorry for some of you who may not be happy with some of the ideas I have described. I cannot make everyone happy; it could be your bad karma due to your greediness or ego. The rules of karma will work on you and your family because you are connected.

Please forgive my big mouth because I love you from the bottom of my heart with unconditional love.

**We are one.**

**We are the people to make changes.**

**We are the people responsible for the changes.**

**We are the people, the majority, and we are all connected to one another in this cyber era.**

**Get connected with your God to love others.**

**This is the year for a new cycle! We evolve our culture with new ideas.**

**Take action for the changes.**

Go figure! Your brain is acting as a symbol of infinity.

Let's start another new beginning!

Let's save this country and our president, starting with health care.

Move on to tax rates, housing, employment, and education.

Get connected with your friends, family, colleagues by Face book or LinkedIn, Twitters, e-mails, etc.!

Get as many people as you know involved.

Trust in yourself that you are powerful and can make changes.

Have fun with your congressman!

# Epilogue

My apology for the delay as I expected to publish this book much sooner. I was so overwhelmed over this task and I had so much hesitancy. I also told you I am not quite punctual and wait for the last minute. I was also involved in a car accident while I was stopped at a signal and my car was rear-ended in 2012.

When I was rejected for health insurance due to a preexisting condition a few years ago, I felt I was on a big string band stretched across the Pacific Ocean. I was lucky because I was covered by the national health insurance in my home country. I also felt the insurance system in this country does not treat a person as a human. When I came back, the majority of my patients were gone after a few months. I was feeling I was trashed in the garbage can because of this insurance system. I decided to open up my big mouth rather than staying in the pity pot. As I was working on my papers over the past several years to submit to chiropractic journals for free, I decided to publish to let the public know how the body works and how chiropractic works on your body. The weird bird came to me and I realized that I have invisible wings. I believe everyone has invisible wings like I do. When you are ready to fly, you will . . . such as leaving your parents' house to go to college or to get married. I finally flew by writing this book. It was my *Out on a Limb* by Shirley McLain that is also a good book. I am getting tired of travelling back and forth to my home country to get adequate health care at an affordable rate and am getting sick of hearing complaints about this US health care system.

Even though I liked the Olympic opening ceremony in Beijing in 2008, with all the man power and the beautiful performances by teamwork, the London Olympics in 2012 were very symbolic to me as they started labor's revolutions and child care to treat people as human beings in the opening ceremony. John Lennon's, "Imagine," in the closing ceremony was also very symbolic to me. I am a dreamer; however, a dream makes a person stronger to walk toward the goal. One person may not have enough power, but one person can work for thousands and thousands can work for one. As I am bilingual and have lived in a different country, I understand the differences between the two and could collect the information from different viewpoints. To obtain different viewpoints is spiritual growth. Patients' viewpoints are different from doctors' viewpoints. Saving a person's life is a tough duty and worth a $1 million or priceless by a state of the art surgery; however, paying $1 million by one person is too much of a burden. That's why I took mid-points such as a national insurance system and proactive care.

Fundraising and donations are also characteristic in this country and we don't know how the money is spent.

I received an email on different CEOs income including the Red Cross. We may need to create different agencies to publish how money is spent from donation rather than sending out junk mail and wasting so much paper. I would "Go Green" to pamper nature. I don't say I don't tell lies, but I keep my promise. I would plant trees for paper copies of my book.

My nicknames change from time to time; I chose this pen name as a female version of Michael Moore. As I told you, women go into more details. There are only men and women on earth, no matter what type of sexual orientation you have. Loving and caring for each other is the most beautiful part of human nature. Science is starting to reveal some of the changes in DNA for one's sexual orientations. I heard there is a major sexual switch in souls since the last century. We are from different planets and have different orientations. I am a woman from Venus. I found another interesting website to communicate with entities from different planets. It is www.ladyashtar.com.

Return to the origin.

Be myself.

Select what I need are my principles for my life.

I select love, peace, and harmony.

I smoke American Spirits cigarettes for my stress management; I am patriotic. My sensitivity drives me crazy and I want to mask the sensitivity. I also want to know how the body connects to each other and it helps me to swallow tears in this non-stop violence with discriminations. Those are my excuses for my bad habit. As I am a snail, I don't think I am a loser because I created those theories over several years.

Oh men, I am bold, no bra to enjoy my freedom and smoking like a man.

I told you karma comes back!

My website is www.drmichellemoore.com. All copyrights are reserved by Dr. Michelle Moore, DC.

*If you loved this book, would you please provide a review at Amazon.com?*

# Resources

Textbook of Medical Physiology 8th edition by Guyton

Atlas of Human Anatomy by Netter

Gray's Anatomy

Principle of Neural Science 4th edition by Erick Kendal and James H. Schwartz

Neurological Differential Diagnosis 2nd edition by John Pattern

Carrick Institute graduate study for neurology class notes

Numerous SOT manuals by Major B. DeJarnette

The Art of Chiropractic by M. L. Rees

Cranial Sutures, Analysis, Morphology and manipulative strategies by Marc Pick

Cranial and meningeal motion DVD by Dr. Marc Pick

Rebirthing